MARY ROBINSON

A President with a Purpose

FERGUS FINLAY

THE O'BRIEN PRESS
DUBLIN

First published 1990 by The O'Brien Press Ltd.,
20 Victoria Road, Dublin 6, Ireland.

10 9 8 7 6 5 4 3 2

British Library Cataloguing in Publication Data

Finlay, Fergus
Mary Robinson: a president with a purpose.
1. Elections
I. Title
324.9417

ISBN 0-86278-257-0

Cover design: Michael O'Brien
Typesetting: The O'Brien Press
Separations: The City Office, Dublin.
Printing: Colour Books, Ltd., Dublin.

Mary Robinson

A President with a Purpose

"... will be a woman candidate for the Park for the first time the institution of the presidency was established. Very much utsider, Mrs Robinson will be aiming at a good showing, as no realistic chance of winning out at the end of the day ..."

Sunday Press, April 8th, 1990

"...we are going to win – as I believe we can – it is going to call a truly heroic effort and total commitment to the task. It ll be worth the effort, because to return an elected working President supported by a mandate from the people will literally change the shape of Irish politics and signal a more open and pluralistic society."

Letter from Mary Robinson to supporters, June 1990

"I was elected by men and women of all parties and none, by many with great moral courage who stepped out from the faded flags of the Civil War and voted for a new Ireland. And above all by the women of Ireland – Mná na hÉireann – who instead of rocking the cradle rocked the system, and who came out massively to make their mark on the ballot paper, and on a new Ireland."

Mary Robinson's acceptance speech after she was declared elected, RDS, Dublin, 9th November, 1990

President Mary Robinson

With the quill used by Eamon De Valera, Mary Robinson signs the Declaration of Office at the inauguration ceremony, St Patrick's Hall, Dublin Castle, 3rd December, 1990. At this moment she became Ireland's new President. (Independent Newspapers)

CONTENTS

Dedicated to Mandy, a Robinson fan

ACKNOWLEDGEMENTS

I would like to thank the following for their help (under pressure!) in getting this book finished so quickly. All the members of the committee were very helpful, both in checking facts and in jogging my memory. Dick Walsh and *The Irish Times* helped me with information; and John Foley and *The Irish Independent* helped with figures. Ide O'Leary worked extremely hard to help make it accurate and readable. Dick Spring gave me the time off and the encouragement without which this book wouldn't have been possible; and Frieda and the girls kept the coffee coming.

Nobody who helped me should be held responsible for any errors in the book – they're all my own.

Fergus Finlay

To produce a book like this in such a short time required great commitment. We received help from many quarters. A special thanks to Peter MacMenamin for his humour, calmness and hard work.

Many people helped with the illustrations and gave freely in the spirit of the Robinson campaign. I am grateful to Brenda O'Hanlon who helped organise these. Thank you Paddy Barker of *The Cork Examiner*, Dermot O'Shea, Peter Thursfield and Rosaleen Bamford of *The Irish Times*, Pat Keegan and Brian Barron of *The Irish Press*, Dave Halloran, Padraig Beirne and Frank McGrath of Independent Newspapers, Henry Wills of *The Western People*.

Thanks to Finn Gillespie for the photograph on page 74 (top) and our friends at The Blackstaff Press for permission to quote from "Backside to the Wind", by Paul Durcan.

I congratulate and thank the O'Brien Press team for the magnificent work in producing this book in record time. A special thanks to Liz Meldon, Ivan O'Brien and Ide O'Leary for taking on a big challenge. Thanks also to Declan Maguire of The City Office and John Harold of Colour Books for a speedy and high quality production.

We are also grateful to Dave Mullins of the *Sunday World*, Eamonn Farrell of Photocall, James Meehan of Inpho, Michael Brophy of *The Star* and F.X.Martin.

Michael O'Brien

Introduction

On the 9th of November 1990, Mary Robinson was declared elected President of Ireland.

It had been clear since the middle of the previous day, as the tally returns started coming in from around the country, that she was going to make it. The most pessimistic forecasts at the end of the first count had her winning by a margin of perhaps 50,000 votes once Austin Currie's second preference votes were distributed. In the event, her margin of victory over Brian Lenihan, often described as the most popular politician in Ireland, was 86,000 votes, a huge mandate by any standards.

But the best was yet to come. Standing on a small wooden platform in the middle of the main hall of the RDS, surrounded by hundreds of people who had worked for her for much of the previous six months, she delivered a speech that was to send an echo right around the country. Ironically, the speech was broadcast live on RTE Radio during the Angelus at 6 p.m. One of the first consequences of her election was the displacement of the traditional prayer!

No-one who was there will ever forget the feeling of pure unadulterated joy that speech evoked. Delivered in her characteristically strong voice, it was full of resonances of the campaign itself, and of the future. As much even as the *fact* of her victory, the speech she made in victory assured everyone who was listening that things would never be quite the same again.

This is what she said:

Exactly one year ago today, the Berlin Wall came down. Five months later, at the invitation of the Labour Party, I applied to the people of Ireland for the job of President. They said: "Don't ring us, we'll ring you." In other words, show us you are serious. The task ahead seemed daunting but straightforward enough in the quiet of my study. The tradition of easy-going elections, or indeed no elections for the presidency, seemed to promise a fairly sedate seven months. In theory, I would put a comprehensive and constructive case for a working presidency before the people in a rational and responsible fashion, and on the basis of the policies put forward the Irish people would decide. The political soothsayers predicted the Irish people would give me a vote commensurate with that of the parties supporting me – in other words, third place.

I began my campaign in May in places like Limerick, Allihies in West Cork, the Inishowen Peninsula and the islands of the west coast, in a journey of joy and discovery of myself, of my country, of the people of Ireland. Now seven months later I find that these places did not forget me. The people of Ireland did ring me, and you gave me the job, and I don't know whether to dance or sing – and I have done both. That seven months seems like seven years. There was nothing rational or reasonable about the campaign which developed into a barnstorming, no-holds-barred battle between my *ad hoc* assembly of political activists, amateurs, idealists and romantic realists against the might, money and merciless onslaught of the greatest political party on this island. And we beat them!

Today is a day of victory and valediction. Even as I salute my supporters as Mary Robinson, I must also bid them farewell as President-elect. They are not just partisans, but patriots too. They know that as President of Ireland, I must be a President for all the people. More than that, I *want* to be a President for all the people. Because I was elected by men and women of all parties and none, by many with great moral courage who stepped out from the faded flags of the Civil War and voted for a new Ireland. And above all by the women of Ireland – *Mná na hÉireann!* – who instead of rocking the cradle rocked the system, and who came out massively to make their mark on the ballot paper, and on a new Ireland.

Some say a politician's promises are worthless. We shall see. I mean to prove the cynics wrong. What I promised as candidate I mean to deliver as President. Áras an Uachtaráin will, to the best of my ability, become a home as well as a house – a home for all those aspirations of equality and excellence which have no other home in public life. The first step in that process is to preserve and protect the building itself, and one of my first acts as President will be to consult with An Taoiseach, whose regard and respect for our arts and heritage I admire and acknowledge, and whom I know will give this aspect of affairs his best attention. But the material fabric is only the envelope of the enterprise, of that quest for equality and excellence of which I mean the presidency to be the symbol.

I have a mandate for a changed approach within our Constitution. I spoke openly of change and I was elected on a platform of change. I was elected not by the parties of Ireland but by the people of Ireland, people of all parties. I will be a President of all the people, a symbol of reconciliation as well as renewal, not least in my commitment to pluralism and peace on this island. But I am not just a President of those here today but of those who cannot be here; and there will always be a light on in Áras an Uachtaráin for our exiles and our emigrants – those of whom the poet Paul Durcan so movingly wrote:

> Yet I have no choice but to leave, to leave,
> And yet there is nowhere I more yearn to live
> Than in my own wild countryside,
> Backside to the wind.

But as well as our emigrants abroad we have exiles at home – all those who are at home but homeless: the poor, the sick, the old, the unemployed, and above all the women of Ireland who are still struggling on the long march to equality and equity.

To all those who have no voice or whose voice is weak, I say: Take heart. There is hope. Look what you did in this election. You made history. As President I hope we will make history together. *Dóchas linn Naomh Pádraig – agus treise libh Mná na hÉireann – a bhúail buille, ní amháin ar bhur son féin, ach ar son cheart an duine!"*

The speech was interrupted a number of times by ecstatic applause. Especially when the phrase *"Mná na hÉireann"* rang out, it seemed that the roof of the RDS would lift off. By the time she had finished, many in the hall were crying, including some who would normally regard themselves as among the hard-bitten cynics of Irish politics. The same thing happened all around the country when substantial excerpts from the speech were played on the Nine O'Clock News that night. And it was by no means women who did all the crying. Dick Spring, who had originally nominated Mary Robinson, said privately later that he was very glad he had spoken before Mary's speech, because he was unable to say more than a few words after it.

People cried that day out of a feeling of the most intense exhilaration. There are very few occasions in politics when that feeling is evident among so many, or is as public as it was at that moment. Politics is made up of private moments – private grief and private triumph – but only once or twice in a lifetime is it possible for so many people to share in the joy of so crucial a victory.

It was triumph without triumphalism, because the victory belonged to everybody. It was a sense that history had been made, and more – that history was going to go on being made. The impossible had been achieved, and nothing was going to be impossible ever again. For women – and men – all over Ireland, the future began at the moment that Mary Robinson was elected.

But the office to which she was elected had up to then been seen as a nonentity. Again and again throughout the campaign, Mary had been told by people sympathetic to her cause that she would be wasted "up in the Park". A non-executive President, devoid of practical power, could achieve little by way of the kind of radical change that Mary Robinson had always sought, and had always represented. The history of the presidency was full of men content to serve as figureheads. The office had become meaningless.

So how did all that change with the election of Mary Robinson? Why did so many people invest so much effort into securing this "sinecure" for her? Why did it become so crucial – and why, in the end, has her election threatened to change the whole nature of Irish politics so fundamentally?

One possible answer lies in the "journey of joy and discovery" that Mary Robinson undertook to secure election to an office that initially she did not want. Mary Robinson did not just discover Ireland in the seven months of her campaign – Ireland discovered her, and much more importantly, Ireland with her help discovered new things about itself.

"In the quiet of my study"

At any time of the year Ballydavid, near Dingle, can be a beautiful but lonely place. On the 5th of January, it is isolated and bleak. Not the sort of place where one would consider starting a successful campaign to take the presidency away from the grip of Fianna Fáil.

Yet that was precisely what Dick Spring had in mind that day as he drove to Ballydavid to record an interview with Shane Kenny for the News at One on RTE. Raidio na Gaeltachta has a studio there, and it was agreed that Spring would record the interview from the remote studio rather than going to one of RTE's regional locations in Cork or Limerick. It was still the Christmas break, after all, and there wasn't a lot of news around. That was one of the reasons why Kenny had lined up a series of interviews with the leaders of the various political parties in the Dáil, asking them to outline their plans and ambitions for the coming year.

Dick Spring had been convinced for a long time that the presidency should be seriously contested. It had been a source of considerable regret to him that he had not felt able to put forward a candidate in 1983, because he had been in Government at the time, and because the Government as a whole was anxious not to be involved in a contest. Besides, the then incumbent, President Hillery, was willing, albeit reluctantly, to serve a second term, provided it was as an agreed candidate. Anyone wishing to see the office contested in 1983 would have faced the accusation that he had forced the resignation of the sitting President, since Hillery would not have contested.

Things were different now. In the first place, President Hillery, even if he wanted one, was constitutionally debarred from a third term. Secondly, Spring was in opposition, and had spent the previous two years building an independent profile for the Labour Party. Several times in the preceding couple of months he had raised the subject of a possible presidential election with his Parliamentary Party, and they had given him a free hand to take whatever action he deemed appropriate.

But Dick Spring was not the first person to whom it had occurred that a presidential election was due in 1990. PJ Mara, the Government's chief spokesman, had already begun to work on the subject. Using carefully constructed leaks and a number of interested journalists, he had planted the idea that Brian Lenihan would make an excellent President for the country. In the run up to Christmas, it had appeared in a sufficient number of newspapers for RTE to become interested and to interview the Tánaiste about it. Although disclaiming any campaign for the office, he had told RTE that if elected, he would be proud and honoured to serve.

This had all the appearance of a set-up, a plan to ensure that not only would no other Fianna Fáil candidate for the office get an opportunity to emerge, but that other parties would be sufficiently intimidated by Lenihan's obvious popularity that they would be forced to agree to nominate him unopposed.

Clearly, taking him on in a contest *would* be difficult. Not only was he among the most popular politicians in the country, he had acquired the status of a virtual folk hero in the way in which he had confronted and apparently beaten a crippling disease, and had been the first politician elected in the general election of 1989 even though he was still recovering in an American hospital from a liver transplant operation.

Besides, no-one had ever beaten Fianna Fáil in a presidential election before, and with that party riding high in opinion polls, it seemed unlikely that anyone would want to take them on this time. Fine Gael, the largest opposition party, had substantial difficulties of its own, and Spring believed that if he did not mount a challenge, no-one would. And it was vital, in Dick Spring's view, that the office should be contested. The presidency had been designed, after all, as an office directly elected by the people. No other office in the Constitution carried such a direct mandate. In Spring's view, it was the capacity of the people to elect their own President that was the only thing that gave the office meaning. He believed that he should either be campaigning for the abolition of the office, or to make it relevant again by giving the people a choice.

In addition, he believed strongly that the presidential election could be used as an opportunity to debate the future direction of the country, and to tap into the vote for change that he was convinced existed. The country had been through two bruising and divisive referenda – one about abortion, the other about divorce – and a number of general elections. Spring believed that the net effect of the political developments of the last few years had been the beginning of the emergence of a two-tier society in Ireland, with Government policy increasingly geared towards solving financial problems at the expense of essential social services, and with politicians generally seeking to bury controversial moral issues. The presidential election was a vital opportunity to assess the strength of the vote for change in the country.

But who is likely to take seriously the leader of a party that habitually secures 10 per cent of the vote if he says he is going to nominate a candidate capable of beating Fianna Fáil, which in recent years has never got less than 42 per cent of the national vote in any election?

That was the question on Spring's mind as he drove to Dingle that morning. Before leaving Tralee, he had told Shane Kenny that he was going to raise the subject of the presidency in the course of the interview, and a couple of days previously, he had asked his staff to prepare some notes on the office of the presidency and all the reasons why there should be an election. As he looked back over these notes, he realised that they were worthy, but not newsworthy. If he was to talk about democracy and the will of the people, no-one would disagree, but very few would remember it the following day. He decided to give Shane Kenny a real news item instead, something that would make the interview memorable.

A number of Spring's associates had tuned into the news that day, expecting to hear the party leader talk about the presidential election, among other things. What he actually said made them sit bolt upright. Not only was he determined to ensure that there would be an election for the office of President this year, but if necessary, he told an obviously surprised Shane Kenny, he would go forward himself as a candidate in order to ensure that one took place.

Within the Labour Party, his remarks caused consternation. He himself was unavailable for the rest of the day, since he had taken his family with him to Dingle, and they didn't return to Tralee until late that evening. When they came back, it was to be told that every newspaper in the country had been enquiring about whether or not he had completely lost his marbles.

A number of them decided they knew the answer already. The *Cork Examiner*, for instance, in a stinging editorial the following morning, gave vent to the view that Spring obviously didn't take the presidency, or his present job, or the party that had elected him as its leader, seriously at all. He couldn't be regarded as remotely qualified, "De Paper" argued – he was far too young, and still had a political career in front of him. If he persisted with this nonsense, he would lose the credibility that he had been trying to build up over years.

Other newspapers followed suit, all of them pointing out that the presidency was traditionally reserved for a senior (usually elderly) man who had served a long apprenticeship. Not one newspaper was prepared to accept that the time had come to break the presidential mould. But Dick Spring had nevertheless secured his first objective: the newspapers and the rest of the media were already gearing themselves to the certainty that there would be an election. The "shooing-in" of Brian Lenihan had stopped.

The second objective was likely to be a lot more difficult. Dick Spring analysed the problem this way, in a meeting with some of his staff three days later: the candidate who runs against Brian Lenihan, and presumably against Fine Gael as well, must be someone whose appeal stretches beyond the traditional confines of the Labour Party. (At that time, it was impossible even to presume the support of the Workers' Party, since they had been angered by remarks that Spring had made about their difficulties arising from the collapse of communism in Eastern Europe, and were insisting that any candidate who would seek to represent the left would have to be chosen by them as well as by Labour.) The candidate must also be someone who clearly represented a desire for progressive change.

Finally, Spring insisted, it must be someone young enough and strong enough to be prepared to campaign long and hard for the job, since that was the only possible way in which sufficient votes could be garnered to keep a candidacy alive against the big guns of Fianna Fáil and Fine Gael.

No names were discussed at that meeting, and no clear ideas as to where a candidate might come from emerged. What was decided was to draw up a "job description" which would more clearly set out the different ideas in circulation about a new role for the President. Rather than try to draw up a list of those who might be sounded out on the idea of running, Spring wanted to see the sort of campaign that could be put together, believing that a name might naturally emerge from that process – or at least, that a lot of other names might be eliminated.

Two people were put to work on this "job description", John Rogers and Fergus Finlay, Dick Spring's assistant. John Rogers, a former Attorney General and a close friend and advisor of Spring, introduced a number of ideas on which he had been working about possible changes in the constitutional role of the President. These were based on the general idea of "a working presidency", and included, among other things, the notion of radical reform of the Senate to broaden its franchise (which would be possible to do under law) and to have the President as ex-officio Chair. Fergus Finlay added ideas on a social role for the presidency, to incorporate the concept of the President as a "voice for the voiceless".

A couple of days later, while this work was going on in some secrecy, Denise Rogers, Ruairi Quinn's secretary, expressed the opinion one morning that Dick Spring couldn't possibly run for the Park, as he still had a lot of work to do as leader of the Labour Party. "The only one we should consider asking," she said, "is Mary Robinson. She's someone who could really make a difference if she was elected."

Dick Spring had been adamant from the first moment the matter had been discussed that it was essential that the candidate selected by

Labour should be the first to be formally nominated, and should be prepared to campaign hard around the length and breadth of Ireland for as long as it took. With three candidates likely to be contesting at the end of the day, the only things possible to predict were that the Fianna Fáil candidate would get somewhere in excess of 40 per cent of the vote, and the Labour candidate would start from a position of being in third place. But it was to be an election fought on the basis of proportional representation, and in that situation, the candidate who came in second on the first count could cause a major upset. Coming in second was possible, in Spring's view, but only with six months' hard work by the person chosen.

The remark made by Denise Rogers found its way back to John Rogers (no relation), who thought long and hard about it. The "job description", by then almost complete, read as if it had been tailor-made for Mary Robinson. As a former senator and a constitutional lawyer, she could be relied on to understand intimately the proposals for a working presidency. As someone with a long track record in using the law to defend and advance the interests of minorities and of oppressed individuals, she fitted neatly into the notion of "a voice for the voiceless". As someone who was young, and well-known, as well as being an attractive personality in her own right, she had the potential to attract a large personal following. And it was undeniable that her election, even her candidature, would change forever the nature of the debate about the office of President.

But there were also problems in his view. Mary Robinson would have to be sold first and foremost to the Labour Party, for it was the party that would have to nominate her. And she had resigned from Labour some five years earlier, in a major row about the Anglo-Irish Agreement. She had chosen to retire from public life after the general election the previous summer, and was now both busy and successful in her law practice and in the Irish Centre for European Law. She wouldn't be likely to feel that she owed the Labour Party anything – if the idea didn't appeal to her on its own merit, she would certainly say No. And it would damage Dick Spring's credibility if the first person he approached were to turn him down, especially if that person was not even a member of the Party.

There was one other problem – there were by now two other candidates apparently willing to offer themselves. One was Dr Noel Browne, who had been approached after Spring's radio interview by a number of members of the Labour left faction of the party, apparently intent on upstaging Spring by producing a candidate of their own. Those familiar with the set of ideas that Spring was quietly developing, felt that Browne was quite unsuitable as a candidate. They were convinced that he would not have the discipline or stamina to undertake the kind of campaign that the Labour leader had in mind. But some members of the party were busy trying to achieve a *fait accompli* for Browne, and speed was now becoming important. In addition, the Workers' Party were letting it be known that they would like to see Dr John deCourcy Ireland receive the joint nomination of the left. DeCourcy Ireland is a distinguished maritime historian who has been associated with left-wing causes all his life, but has never achieved the kind of national profile that would be necessary to secure second place in the election. He too simply did not fit into Spring's plan.

With all these considerations in mind, John Rogers approached Mary Robinson in February (on Valentine's Day!), telling her that he would like to discuss some ideas about the presidency with her. They met later the same day in her house.

Rogers had brought with him the paper containing the set of constitutional ideas that he had been working on, adding up to a radically different concept of a working presidency. Mary Robinson read it with interest, and also with something approaching horror. She realised immediately that John Rogers was not here looking for legal advice about these ideas, but that his purpose was to interest her personally in them. There could only be one reason. Without putting it into words, he was asking her to consider the possibility of campaigning for the idea – in other words, for the office itself.

She was shaken, and said so. She had put campaigning politics behind her, and had embarked on a new phase of her life. He pointed out that if the ideas were worthwhile – and she agreed that they were

– someone suitably qualified would have to put their weight behind them. Otherwise, the presidency would continue to be a stultified sinecure, with little or no relevance to the people of the country. And who was better qualified, legally and in terms of a track record, than she?

After that first meeting, John Rogers left Mary Robinson's house uncertain as to whether she was more fascinated or repelled by the seed he had sown. At no stage had he given her the impression that he had the nomination for the presidency in his gift. On the other hand, she now knew that if she wanted, she could make herself a serious candidate for consideration.

As for Mary Robinson, she had never contemplated the idea of running for the presidency. Like many others, she regarded the office as something totally underdeveloped that had grown into a reward for loyal service, something available only to the politician or other dignitary chosen by Fianna Fáil. In essence she had never thought of the presidency as an office capable of making much of a difference. And Mary Robinson's career had always been about making a difference.

Over the next few days, though, she found it hard to suppress a surge of excitement every time the thought of putting her hat into the ring came up. She found that she was being attracted by two things. The first was the powerful symbolism inherent in the notion of a woman running for – and winning – the highest office in the land. In a country that had never had a woman in the Supreme Court, or in the highest constitutional offices, and where women had been damaged over the years by the subservience of their position, the election of a woman to the presidency would represent an enormous breakthrough. Like many others, Mary Robinson still remembered the pain suffered by thousands in the course of the two referendum campaigns. Surely this was a chance to undo some of that damage.

The second appeal was the opportunity of being involved in a campaign that would provide a national stage for things that needed to be said, changes that needed to be made. Even if it wasn't winnable in the end, wasn't the presidency worth fighting for? Wasn't it important that no one group should feel free to regard the only office in the country elected by every citizen over the age of eighteen as their private property? Couldn't people be made to matter, as they hadn't mattered for seventeen years where the presidency was concerned?

When Mary Robinson asked to see John Rogers again a few days later, he knew that she was vitally interested in the whole idea. This time they discussed fully the possibility of Mary running, and went through what would be required in order to secure the nomination. Rogers made sure that no illusions were created – he told her frankly that there would be objections, and that she would have to undergo the same decision-making process as anyone else. But the main thing was – if selected, she was willing to consider running. Rogers agreed to set up a meeting with Dick Spring.

It had been agreed some time earlier by the Parliamentary Labour Party that the decision on who the candidate should be would be a matter for a joint meeting of the party's deputies and senators with the Administrative Council of the party. Even though, under the Constitution, only members of the Oireachtas are entitled to nominate a candidate for the presidency, Spring's feeling was that a person chosen by the whole party would more readily secure the backing of the whole party. And only the Administrative Council could commit money and other party resources to a campaign.

When Dick Spring and Mary Robinson met in the middle of March, that procedure was among the first things he explained. The meeting took place in Mary's house in Sandford Road, at the end of a long working day for everyone present. There were six people at the meeting: Mary and Nick Robinson, together with Bride Rosney, a close friend who was to become a key strategist behind the campaign, Spring, Rogers, and Fergus Finlay. The meeting lasted until the early hours of the morning.

Dick Spring made it clear to Mary Robinson that he was prepared to nominate her at the next meeting of the Administrative Council, which would be convened jointly with the Parliamentary Party for the purpose of selecting a candidate, and that if selected, she would then be the official candidate of the party. It would be up to them to decide in the final analysis, rather than up to him. He went on to tell her that he saw it as his and the party's role to build as strong a consensus around her as possible – and to that end, he would be actively seeking the support of not only other parties on the left, but of a wide range of groups and individuals in society. Mary, for her part, would be expected to be a candidate for a working, caring presidency, and would have to agree to undertake perhaps the longest and most physically demanding campaign that had ever been contemplated in Irish politics.

On one point there was a long and contentious discussion – on the issue of Mary's membership of the party. Spring pointed out to her that she would be a lot easier to "sell" internally if she was to agree to rejoin. Mary, however, was adamant. She would not rejoin the party, because she was not prepared to be seen as someone who would abandon an independent position simply to secure a nomination. She had taken a principled stand in resigning from the party five years earlier, and she could not go back on that now. Besides, she argued, was it not much more likely that a consensus could be built that was broader than the party's core support, if the candidate was seen as not beholden to any organisation? She wanted to be, she said, the Labour Party candidate, with a capacity to reach constituencies where the party had only limited appeal.

Despite misgivings, Spring accepted this point, though it took several further meetings to resolve it. He was reassured by Mary's affirmation that she had more in common, in policy terms, with the Labour Party than with any other party, and that her objection to joining was not based on antagonism to the party, but rather on the need to preserve a sense of independence for the sake of her own integrity and the prospects of a successful campaign. If she won the election – and she was committing herself to this campaign on the clear understanding that she was in it to win – she would be debarred from any involvement in any political party. Spring agreed that in a situation where the prize was an office outside party politics, the appeal of an independent-minded candidate could transcend that of anyone seen purely as a party loyalist. Besides, the option of rejoining the party could arise only if she didn't become President but she had indicated she had no intention of doing so.

Up to now, all the discussions about Mary Robinson's possible candidature had taken place in secret. There were a number of reasons for this – the principal one was Dick Spring's desire that Labour should be the first in the field with a nominated choice. He was convinced that the chances of doing well depended on stealing a march on the larger political parties. Fianna Fáil were still talking about the presidency and Brian Lenihan (with one or two others as possible, though unlikely contenders), but had gone nowhere near making a formal decision. The Fine Gael leader Alan Dukes had told his party's Árd Fheis that they would be contesting the election with a candidate of substance, and immediately caused widespread confusion in party ranks, with the majority of party members assuming that Garret FitzGerald would run, and with FitzGerald having to explain a number of times that he was not available. Spring believed that if anyone became aware that he was contemplating nominating a woman, and a young woman at that, it would open up options for the other parties, especially Fine Gael.

At the same time, the campaign for Noel Browne was gathering some momentum within the Labour Party. Letters were being circulated on behalf of his candidacy, and it was attracting a degree of publicity. After consulting a number of members of the Parliamentary Party, Spring decided to move quickly.

At a meeting of the Parliamentary Party on April the 4th the party leader unveiled his plan. He told the meeting that he was seeking their approval to invite Mary Robinson to stand for the presidency on behalf of the party. He had every reason to believe that she would accept such an invitation, and if she did, he would be placing her name, and no other, before the joint meeting due to be held at the end of the month. The minutes of that meeting show that the idea was accepted with universal acclamation, and with no dissenting voice.

Some sensitivity was expressed about the position of Noel Browne, and it was agreed that the party leader should ring him before any announcement was made. It was felt that if the position was made fully clear to him, he could be an asset for Mary Robinson in the ensuing campaign. Apart from that, there was a general feeling at the meeting that the choice of Mary Robinson would put the party in with a real chance of fighting a meaningful campaign.

Immediately after the meeting, Spring did two things. First, he tried to contact Proinsias De Rossa, leader of the Workers' Party, to tell him what had transpired, and to ask for his support for Mary's candidacy. Learning that he was at a meeting of the European Parliament in Strasbourg, Spring faxed him the news there, in the hope that De Rossa would hear it first from him rather than from the newspapers. Second, he rang Noel Browne at his home in Connemara. It didn't go well. The party leader explained that the nature of the campaign he was proposing to run was radically different to any that had been run in the past, and required a candidate with a very particular set of qualifications. For this reason, he said, the candidate who had emerged from his consideration was Mary Robinson. Browne received this news in total silence, thanked Spring tersely for the call, and hung up.

The party leader then issued a public statement, saying that he had received the authority of the Parliamentary Party to invite Mary Robinson to stand for selection by the Administrative Council, and extolling her virtues as a candidate. Immediately, all hell broke loose. Despite the clear understanding of most people present at the Parliamentary Party meeting, one of the party's deputies, Emmet Stagg, issued a statement saying that no such authority had been given to the leader, who was trying to pre-empt proper debate within the party. This version was supported, after a fashion, by Michael D Higgins. When Mary Robinson met the press later in the day on the steps of Leinster House, she was confronted with a major internal party row, rather than with the consensus which everyone agreed was essential to success.

She was intensely annoyed, believing that her candidacy had been allowed to get off to the worst possible start. Outwardly however she maintained perfect composure for the next three weeks, insisting that she was fully prepared to accept the democratic decision of the party at the end of the day. Browne waited less gracefully, and made a number of disparaging remarks about her in the course of a Today Tonight interview before the Administrative Council meeting which was to decide between them (when Mary was asked in a similar interview whether or not she would support Browne's candidacy if he were chosen instead of her, she replied simply "Of course").

The Administrative Council meeting took place on April 26th in an atmosphere of tension. Some time prior to the meeting, a statement had been issued carrying the names of two members of Labour left which accused the party leader of effectively telling lies in his account of the events leading up to the meeting. Spring decided that it was not appropriate to deal with this statement at the meeting itself, and that every effort should be made to ensure that the decision about the candidate was reached in the most dignified way possible. The result was a series of low key speeches which avoided recrimination and simply put forward the case for the two opposing candidates. Robinson was nominated by Spring, and seconded by Niamh Bhreathnach, who had herself been the first woman elected to the office of Vice-chairperson of the party. After similar speeches in support of Browne, a vote was taken.

The result was announced less than an hour after the start of the meeting. Mary Robinson was the official candidate of the Labour Party, by a majority of three to one. Immediately, the party closed ranks. Both Michael D Higgins and Emmet Stagg let it be known that despite their earlier positions, Mary Robinson would have their full support (and both of them worked unstintingly for her throughout the campaign).

On Saturday the 7th of April, a few days after her name had become public, Mary Robinson fulfilled a long-standing engagement to address a seminar of the Mayo Women's Group in Castlebar. She had agreed to talk to them many months before on the subject of "Women and the Law", and a room had been booked that could accommodate perhaps fifty women. Several hundred turned up, to meet this Mayo woman who was about to take on the biggest parties in the land.

The journey of joy and discovery had begun.

"A journey of joy and discovery"

Mary Robinson was a lawyer who went into politics – not a politician who studied law. It is that fact more than anything else that has equipped her to pursue the independent line that led her to the Presidency.

If she has spent the last thirty years preparing herself to be President, as the office has been understood up to now, there is very little sign of it. In fact, it might be more correct to say that Ireland has spent the last few years preparing itself for Mary Robinson.

In 1974, Conor Cruise O'Brien accused Mary Robinson of condoning the murder of judges. Sixteen years later, he was to write about what music to the ears it was to be able to use the phrase "President Robinson". In the same year that she had been attacked by Conor Cruise O'Brien, she had had her first major confrontation with Brian Lenihan, then the leader of Fianna Fáil in the Senate, who accused her of being "utterly nonsensical". Sometimes in politics it takes a long time for the wheel to turn full circle, but it always does!

Mary Robinson matured *in* politics, rather than before she *came* to politics, and that makes her unusual. Her entry point to politics makes her unique. The first Catholic ever elected to the Trinity College constituency, and at the time the youngest woman elected to the Senate.

A couple of years earlier, Mary Bourke had come back from the United States, where she had had a fellowship in Harvard. The atmosphere into which she was plunged there was radically different from anything she was used to. It was the era of student activism, and of a growing anti-Vietnam war protest. But it was also the time when the Johnson administration was going to eradicate poverty, establish civil rights irrespective of colour, and end the injustice that had been so characteristic of America. America was a place where young people could expand and develop, where they expected – demanded – the right to be involved. Above all, the right to question.

Mary had been raised in an atmosphere where there were no major questions to ask. Her parents were both doctors, and the family was a comfortable one, well-known in Ballina and the surrounding countryside. It was a sheltered, somewhat patrician upbringing.

The Bourkes were the children from the big house, and she was educated privately, first in a small local school with her brothers, and then, from the age of ten, as a boarder in Mount Anville, an exclusive Dublin school. She spent a year in Paris before going on to Trinity, after her father had secured the permission of the archbishop.

As a youngster, she was tough enough to compete with a set of outgoing and extrovert brothers, and bright enough to win scholarships. But politics never entered into her life. There had been no history of it in the family, and even as a Trinity student, she found the whole subject boring. From the earliest age, the law was what fascinated her. America was what opened her up.

Or perhaps it was the contrast between America – its openness, its idealism at the time – and her couple of years on the western circuit as a junior and often very lonely barrister. In the Dublin courts, a lawyer will attend in court for the cases in which he or she is involved, but on the circuit there is often nothing else to do all day but stay in court and watch other lawyers practising. Young lawyers learned a lot about the law that way, and also about the attitudes of the time. She discovered that because she was a woman, men on the all-male jury were as likely to wink at her as to listen to her. She discovered that because she was young, there was an automatic assumption that she couldn't be any good. And she discovered how miserable the hotel rooms and pubs of the west of Ireland could be in those days.

It was in every sense an eye-opening experience. The clash between the culture she had just come from and relished, which expected young people to get involved and to contribute, and the culture she was now working in, which was hide-bound and traditional, was total. It was both a relief and a challenge to be appointed as Reid Professor of Law in Trinity College, accepted by the authorities as a leading expert in her field – years before the all-male juries of the western circuit would have regarded her as ready.

It is highly unlikely that many of them would have regarded her as ready for the Senate either. According to herself, that came about by chance. Until she was elected, Trinity senators, like a lot of others, were usually venerable, respected institutions. She had been talking to friends about the composition of the Senate and saying that if there was university representation at all, it should surely be representative of all generations of university graduates. They all agreed that there should be a younger senator, but who? Who else but the one who had won debating medals as a Trinity student, who had served as secretary of the students' union, who had presented papers to the Law Society, and who was well-known as being capable of arguing with – and changing the minds of – academics twice her age?

Her parents came to Dublin to support her through that first election – to support her in defeat they thought, since it never occurred to any of them that she would win. Twenty years later, her father was to throw himself into the biggest campaign she ever ran – but by then he had learned never to underestimate his daughter.

Ironically, it was not younger graduates who elected her that first time, since very few of them had bothered to enrol as voters. But elected she was, with a ready-made image as a radical, because she was young, and a feminist, because she was a woman and that was the temper of the time.

In fact she was neither radical nor particularly feminist. What she was was a good lawyer, with a deep interest in constitutional aspects of the law. That made her essentially a fundamentalist, committed to the view that the rights and obligations built into the Constitution were of paramount importance. It has been the thing which has under-pinned her from the very beginning – one of the papers she presented to the Law Society while still a student concerned the capacity of the law as an instrument of social change. In that paper she stressed the areas where the law has no place, such as in the area of private morality, where personal freedom and responsibility provide the guidelines rather that anything on the statute books.

As a lawyer who had made these sharp distinctions for herself, she was in some ways the complete opposite of the politician likely to go far. Her understanding of the law, and her commitment to the personal rights inherent in the Constitution – a commitment which had been honed and sharpened in the United States, where all the great judgements had dwelt on the fundamental importance of personal rights – made her intensely frustrated with the attitudes she found in the legislature to which she was elected.

It was that frustration which was to make her the radical she had not been when she was elected. Six months after her election to the Senate, she was threatening in print to march up and down Kildare Street with a placard saying "I AM UNDER-EMPLOYED". Instead she set about making herself busier. She was already discovering the whole range of issues that the politicians all around her were trying to avoid. To her, it was self-evident that politicians, not bishops, should be responsible for legislating on issues of sexual morality. It was self-evident because that was what all her legal training had told her.

That meant that it was through the political process that decisions must be made about the extent to which the law could regulate the availability of contraceptives; about whether the problem of marriage breakdown could be helped by providing the remedy of divorce; about the operation of censorship; about the promotion of co-education in schools; and about the response to the growing problem of women travelling to England for abortions.

In the beginning, Mary didn't see these as women's issues – she saw them as constitutional, legal issues. She was more concerned with the constitutional right of privacy than with the human right of choice; more involved with the need to separate the legislature from what she saw as extraneous influences than with issues of sexism.

Justice was important to Mary because justice flowed from the law, properly applied. Equality was a matter of justice. But her approach when she entered the Senate was academic rather than militant. It was her experience of the Senate that changed her, rather than any ideology she brought with her into that chamber.

She saw herself as a legislator, operating in an environment where too many of her colleagues were simply not prepared to legislate. So she took a hand – giving newspaper interviews in 1971 where she called for the removal of the divorce ban from the Constitution, and a couple of years later preparing and publishing her own legislation to legalise the sale of contraceptives.

By the time she had published that Bill, she was already becoming known as a radical, simply because she took her concept of law seriously. The introduction of internment in the North of Ireland she saw as an affront to the rule of law, and said so, many times and in public – the most famous occasion being when she shared an anti-internment platform with a number of anti-establishment figures in 1974. It was her attendance at that meeting that drew down on her the wrath of Conor Cruise O'Brien, then a member of the coalition Government, who attacked her liberalism as one-sided, and asserted that in failing to address the threats made to judges in Northern Ireland, and the attacks on a number of them, she was in effect condoning the murder of judges. Although the argument was clearly specious, she was hurt by it, and challenged O'Brien to a radio debate. The result was a clear victory for the thirty-year-old senator over the distinguished academic, historian, and Government minister, and although it took him years to admit it, O'Brien was ever afterwards to harbour a secret and grudging admiration for her.

By the time the real controversy broke over her head, though, Mary had been married for four years to Nicholas, employed at the time as a political cartoonist at *The Irish Times*. She was lucky – the extra stability and protection that marriage provided was able to shield her to a considerable extent from the used condoms and filthy letters that came to the house for weeks after she published her contraceptive Bill.

It was a simple measure, aimed at removing the sale and ownership of a range of contraceptives from the criminal law. Its publication stemmed not only from Mary's conviction that private morality was not a fit subject for criminal legislation, but also from her exasperation with a Government that promised action in the area but was clearly afraid to do anything. Opposition came from all quarters – from the Fianna Fáil opposition in the Senate, led by Senator Brian Lenihan, who regularly fell back on the argument that since the Government had promised legislation already, Mary was just being nonsensical; from the Government, which accused her of trying alternately to embarrass or upstage them; and of course from a range of vested interests, some open, and some which clearly belonged in the undergrowth and expressed their feelings by sending venom through the mail to Mary's home.

Although taken aback by the storm she had started, Mary refused to back off. Her Bill was eventually beaten in the Senate, but on the same day, the Government *was* embarrassed into publishing its own Bill. Although a much milder version than Mary's, it too failed to be passed into law, because the Taoiseach of the day, together with the Minister for Education and three back-bench Government deputies voted against it!

In the same year, Mary was outraged to discover that the Government was considering the postponement of implementing European directives on equal pay. She issued a statement threatening the Government that they could be brought to the European Court on the issue – the first time that her politics and her law combined on a social issue. Mary was now beginning to be very widely regarded as someone who meant what she said, and who was prepared to use her position to force social change.

Over the next fifteen years, nobody was responsible for more social change than she was. And in the process she became convinced that political activism had to go side by side with legal activity. She became involved in more causes, and gradually came to be identified as the leading campaigner of the time on behalf of human rights and minority interests.

Everything she did, every activity she undertook, fitted into the same logic. Whether it was representing women in the claim to the right to sit on juries, or marching for Wood Quay; helping to found the Women's Political Association or taking legal actions to secure equality for married couples within the social welfare code; participating in the Anti-Apartheid movement or chairing meetings of Cherish, the organisation for single parents; attacking the operation of the Special Criminal Court, or opposing the declaration of the State of Emergency in 1976 as a "legal trigger" to enable governments to bring in legislation without constitutional checks – all her activities had the same thread running through them, a burning commitment to the rights of individuals. And if it was possible to dismiss her occasionally as excessively moralistic and "holier-than-thou", it was always admitted that she was incapable of making a distinction between the rights of one individual and another. Travellers, unmarried mothers, homosexuals, students – their rights were indivisible. And there was always a gap to be closed – the gap "between what ought to be and what is".

She took one case ostensibly on her own behalf, and it was to have repercussions for women throughout the public service. There was a widows' and orphans' scheme in operation for senators, guaranteeing that in the event of death the next of kin would be provided for. But it only applied to male senators. Mary took the houses of the Oireachtas and the Department of Finance before an Equality Officer under the equality legislation, and he (he!) found against her. She appealed to a full hearing of the Labour Court, and won hands down. The case compelled the Department to introduce a spouses' scheme, to include widowers as well as widows, and the knock-on effects benefited thousands of women workers.

There were ups and downs, of course, defeats as well as victories. The logic of Mary's position was that she should move from the Senate, which was little more than a platform, to the Dáil, where there was a more realistic chance of pursuing change. She had already joined the Labour Party, and contested two general elections without success. It was said at the time that her campaigning style was poor, and there is no doubt too that she suffered from internal division and back-biting within the party. So she bid farewell to Dáil politics without undue regret, and plunged back into her legal and political work with renewed vigour.

She had always had a great deal of contact with Northern Ireland, with members of both communities. At the time of the collapse of Sunningdale in 1974, she was able to say, with the benefit of extensive knowledge of the North, that "it had failed to be sufficiently attractive to those to whom it had to appeal", pointing out that the Irish Government might well admit some day that they had sought too much at Sunningdale – and got too much. Exactly the same logic led her eleven years later to oppose the Anglo-Irish Agreement. Even though still a Labour Party senator when the Agreement was signed in November 1985, she could not vote for it in the Senate because she believed that it was unworkable and that it could lead to an increase rather than a reduction in violence. Since in opposing the agreement she would be voting against her party, she saw no option but to resign.

That decision was effectively the beginning of her withdrawal from politics. Although she was to contest one more Senate election, in 1987, her mind was already turning towards other areas of activity. She had always been committed to the European ideal, and convinced that Europe was going to shape the future of Ireland. Her decision, with Nick, to establish the Irish Centre for European Law in Trinity College was the start of a new pre-occupation and a growing challenge.

Until it was interrupted by the invitation to become President of Ireland.

Dick Spring had told her that the only way it could be done was to be first, and to work hardest. John Rogers had already approached her to suggest starting in Allihies, in the south-westernmost tip of Ireland, at a conference some friends of his were organising immediately after her nomination was made formal.

Two days after the news broke, Eoghan Harris, a producer at the time with RTE, had written to her to say "This is a 'Discover Ireland' trip. Every so often we have to get to know our changing country all over again. So hit the road ..."

All this advice coincided with Mary's own view. Mary Robinson believes in putting down roots. She had put down roots in the Senate, made her mark in a way that would live on. She had put down roots in the law, and established landmarks by which she would always be known. Discussing the campaign with Nick and Bride Rosney, she decided that she was going to put down roots in Ireland. When she called looking for a vote, people were going to remember that she had been there before. When she needed help, they would know her face.

There were easy things to do – well-to-do friends to call on, fashionable venues to visit, trendy newspapers to appear in. Mary decided not to do any of them. She decided to start her campaign formally with a press conference in Catholic, conservative Limerick, on May Day, but first to take John Rogers up on the invitation of a trip to the furthest away village in Ireland.

They say that when you drive from Dublin to Cork, you're only halfway to Allihies. It's a village with a past based on copper mining; a present based on some fishing and a little tourism (and some of the finest cheese made in Europe); and very little future. If Ireland is on the periphery of Europe, Allihies is on the periphery of Ireland. That's why it was picked as the venue for a conference (on 30 April) about peripheral communities. People had come from the islands, from the peninsulas, from Donegal and the far west, to share their experiences, to plot a strategy for the development of their communities, and – though they didn't know it then – to meet the next President of Ireland.

She listened attentively and with growing interest as problems were outlined by speakers from different parts of the country, noting the frustration side by side with the love of place and community that was evident in all of the contributions. When she was asked to address them, she spoke without a script, and they were impressed with her grasp of the problems, and her commitment to them as individuals. The years of dealing with people living on different sorts of margins had given her an understanding of the way in which people can suffer from isolation, and can be increasingly alienated from the centre.

The insights she shared with the people at that conference were those of a woman brought up in the country, with family connections herself in the Inishowen Peninsula, and of a lawyer committed to the right of the individual to participate fully in his or her community. It made a considerable impact on the group that was present.

That very first meeting made a remarkable impact on Mary too. Again and again in the months afterward she was to refer to her beginning in Allihies. It had given her a deep sense of starting in the real Ireland, of going to a place where high office holders had never been, to mingle with people and to listen, to understand and to share. She was beginning to realise what a powerful role a President could play.

From there, they drove to Tralee, where Dick Spring had organised a meeting of Labour Party members. He had confined it to the membership essentially because he wanted to test their reaction – there was a distinct possibility that some at least would be hostile to a non-party member running on their behalf. He needn't have worried. Mary "fired and inspired" them, according to one report. They were overwhelmed, and it was an hour after the meeting before she had finished shaking hands and receiving their assurances of work and support. Six months later, on November 9th, there was a poetic moment in the RDS when the transfers from Kerry North were the votes that put her over the quota.

And then it was on to Limerick, and the media launch of her campaign. Another surprise awaited her there. Jim Kemmy, Frank Prendergast and other left wing activists, including a member of the Workers' Party, had assembled a comprehensively representative group of women's organisations, youth organisations, and left-wing activists to welcome her and to make their support public. There was a little lesson in news management too, which Mary stored away for future reference. A number of photographers had turned up from local and national newspapers, and they took photographs throughout the press conference. But the only one which appeared the following day was a photograph of Mary using a small mirror to powder her nose before the conference began. The "candid" photograph was much more appealing than the usual boring shots taken at such events.

That very first weekend had taught Mary a lot. Everywhere she went, she had been introduced as "the next President of Ireland", but it was easy to tell that the announcement was made almost as a little joke, and certainly more in hope than in expectation. Themes were beginning to emerge – the association with the periphery (and the insight that you could live on the periphery just as much in Tallaght

34

as in the Beara Peninsula); the positive reaction to the idea of a working presidency; the hunger for change among young people and among women; the sense of wanting to "walk tall" for Ireland.

These themes were not being made up by any marketing gurus back in Dublin – they were coming at Mary from the people she was meeting. And there was no shortage of advice either. At one meeting early in the campaign Mary addressed a crowded meeting in Kilkenny, mostly (though not exclusively) of Labour Party members, and mentioned in passing that despite her twenty years in fairly prominent public life, she had never been in Áras an Uachtaráin. "If I haven't ever been invited," she added, "what chance have people got who've never held any office?"

After the meeting, one old man approached her, and after telling her how much he admired her, added, "I do want to give you a little bit of advice. You shouldn't be telling the people that you've never been in the Áras – you should tell them that you've seen what's going on there, and you're the woman to clean up the mess it's in!"

The themes and messages were being honed and sharpened on a daily basis in those first few months. And changed – Mary quickly picked up a lot of feedback that suggested that people wanted to see the role of the President expanded, but within the existing constitutional parameters. References to possible constitutional changes, and to a role for the President in the Senate, were quietly dropped.

The exercise that Mary was engaged in made this kind of change valid. Everywhere she went, she was listening intently, not trying to impose an agenda for the presidency on anybody, but allowing people to set the agenda, reminding them only when necessary of the limitations on the power of the office. Phrases and sentences recurred again and again among the groups she met: "You mightn't be able to force the Government to do anything, but you'd be in a good position to ask"; "We're down here all alone, trying to help ourselves – when is someone going to identify with us?"; "We think the work we're trying to do is important, but nobody else seems to"; "If the President can't go abroad to visit our emigrants, should the emigrants be invited to visit the President instead?" Because she had decided that she was going to listen, all of these responses made a powerful impact on Mary.

And it was the way in which she assimilated them herself – not any advisor or tactician or handler – that led to the central fact that in the end Mary shaped her own campaign. Advisors could argue among themselves – even scream at each other – about what was best for Mary; but it was Mary who decided. And no-one was better equipped – because Mary had put down her own roots in the soil and in the people of Ireland.

The Ireland that Mary was visiting was an Ireland grappling with unemployment, missing its emigrants, helping its old people to deal with the cutbacks in health care and in library services, running its own playgroups for the children of young working mothers. It was an Ireland where people in their own communities – in West Cork and in Ballymun – were pooling their resources to help each other deal with privation and difficulty. It was an Ireland where the help available to women was coming from other women. It was an Ireland beset with problems, and determined to cope; full of anger, side by side with hope; with loneliness and also with neighbourliness still alive.

Mary began to feel that this was a country she understood, and could identify with. It wasn't the Ireland that was most immediately visible from the Four Courts or from Leinster House – or even from pleasant dinner parties in Ranelagh with close friends, decent wine, and good conversation. But it was real, and it was hers to capture.

Somewhere along that road from May to October, Mary Robinson fell in love with Ireland all over again, with its landscape, its people, its courage, and its humour. Even at her weariest, there was never a time when she didn't feel at home in any part of her own country, and it showed. It was the indefinable thing in Mary that, little by little, people began to respond to. It was new to her – a feeling that she wasn't expecting, and certainly wasn't expecting to sustain her for six months – but as she got used to it, the conviction came that win, lose, or draw, the office she was running for was the office she wanted.

At the start of the campaign, Mary thought she could make a difference. By the time it was over, she *knew* – knew that being President of Ireland mattered, not just to her, but to thousands of Irish people; knew that winning the election was what would validate the trust of people who had come to believe in her concept of the presidency; and knew that she could deliver on that trust. She knew because people listened to her when she said it, and more importantly, because people confided in her when she listened. If she had fallen in love with Ireland, it was clear that Ireland had fallen in love with her. The barriers between a shy, professional, somewhat academic woman and her own country fell away in that six months. She became a President for all the people because there were none of the people that she didn't understand, and none who could fail to understand her.

When the last few weeks started, there was no corner of Ireland where Mary had not already been, listening, commanding respect, gradually seeing that respect turn into affection. That "official" tour was a hard physical grind, but the joy was there throughout, and the discoveries never stopped.

It began in Ballina, her home town, on October 20th. Her brothers Henry and Adrian had promised her a send-off to remember, and they had meant every word of it. She had come the previous night from a rapturous reception in Salthill, and simply couldn't believe the lengths to which her home town had co-operated in the arrangements. Robinson banners hung across every street, Robinson posters looked out of every window, every child in the town seemed to be wearing a Robinson sweat shirt. People were even protecting themselves from the teeming rain with Robinson umbrellas. Experienced observers and reporters had never seen anything quite like it.

The actor Mick Lally – "Miley" from the TV series Glenroe – had agreed to give her a send-off from the platform that had been erected at Moylett's Corner. In every direction, the street was packed with people. They were there to see one of their own, a woman who was of the town as much as she was from the town. In that moment, all the politicians and leaders who had made the journey to support her were irrelevant. It was just Mary and her own people.

Mary was not to come back to Ballina until the weekend after she was elected. On the second occasion too, politicians from all parties, and clergymen of all denominations, had gathered to celebrate her. But the central image is still one of Mary among the people she loved best.

Many who had known Mary in previous aspects of her career doubted that she had the personality for the "meet the people" campaign she was going to run. They saw her as too shy and reserved ever to be able to move among people with ease. Some doubted that she had the stamina to undertake so long a journey – 30,000 miles by road over six months. The doubters were forced to eat their words. Mary Robinson opened up to her country in that journey, and she loved every minute of it.

Men on their way to a football match on a Sunday afternoon have no time to be canvassed by a woman. But outside the Sligo Rovers ground one Sunday in October, they crowded around Mary, shaking her hand, smiling, wishing her well.

A week later, Mary walked through the town of Nenagh, late on a Friday afternoon. Out of every shop they came to meet her, lining up on the street, all wanting to hug her and to share a private word. A stop that should have taken ten minutes took an hour.

Early on a miserable Saturday morning, a small group of people lined up near the dock for the Tarbert car ferry. As the ferry came around the headland and the Robinson bus was clearly visible on the flat-bottomed boat, a cheer went up from the waiting people. But at the same time, people began to pour down from the village. It took Mary almost an hour to leave the village, so great was the enthusiasm.

"Why are we stopping here, in the middle of nowhere?" one of the drivers asked as the convoy of cars pulled up high in the mountains between Listowel and Tralee. A small huddle of people waited at the side of the road, ranging in age from four to seventy-four. This was Lyracrumpane, and Mary Robinson was the first presidential candidate who had ever stopped there. She had a word for everyone in the group before the cars sped on, leaving a glow behind them in the winter chill. On polling day, 70 per cent of the votes from the

Lyracrumpane box went to Mary.

In Blarney, a group of people gathered around the campaign bus and began to applaud it. But Mary wasn't on the bus. She was in the Blarney Woollen Mills shop at the time. When one of the tour organisers told the people that Mary would be out soon, they told him that they couldn't wait, since their own bus was about to leave, but they wanted to send her a message anyway.

Everyone loves a winner of course, and as the tour went on, the opinion polls were telling people that Mary was a winner. But it had been many years since walk-abouts and personal appearances had had much influence on elections. Everyone in politics knew that monster meetings were matters for the party faithful, and not occasions for the general public, and that there were ways of ensuring a crowd. For example, in the last week of the campaign Brian Lenihan had been fêted at a huge meeting in Athlone on the night of his dismissal from the Cabinet. It was arranged that way – in the crowd were several hundred people who frequently got casual work in the Department of Education's offices in the town. They had all been "invited" to the meeting by personal letter from Mary O'Rourke, the Minister for Education. Invitations like that are not turned down!

But Mary Robinson's experience was unique. To be sure, the crowds got bigger and more excited as the journey went, but people had been there right from the start – ordinary people, helping Mary to set the agenda by confiding in her, and helping her to set the pace by sharing their problems and their triumphs with her.

That was the biggest discovery of all – that people wanted a President who would be *theirs*, someone in whom they had invested their faith and their hope. Mary never became anyone's property – but by the end of her journey, a little bit of Mary Robinson belonged to everyone.

"Idealists and romantic realists"

Every candidate for political office needs a team around her. She needs to be able to take advice from a wide range of people, and to trust others to deliver on decisions. Especially when a campaign has national implications, the candidate who tries to do everything personally will end up a loser – and will probably burn out on the way.

That's not to say that the candidate can simply hand herself over to a team of handlers and minders, taking no further responsibility for decisions and allowing herself to be packaged and sold like cornflakes. Such an approach would be entirely alien to Mary Robinson's nature. She is, above all, an independent thinker. From the very start of the campaign, she reserved to herself the right to countermand any decision with which she did not agree, and to adjudicate at the end of any process. That was entirely as it should be – a strong candidate must be able to provide the leadership that any team needs, and Mary Robinson led her own campaign from the front. She received advice constantly, and sifted through it carefully – accepting some, rejecting others. When judgement was called for, it was her judgement that ultimately was exercised, on the basis of options put to her by her team. She made mistakes occasionally, and so did the people around her. And she had the capacity to acknowledge mistakes, pick herself up (and encourage anyone else who had stumbled to do likewise) and get on with it.

But she still had to rely on a core group of people to generate a dynamism of their own, and to undertake a wide range of tasks that it would be impossible for the candidate to fulfil – even if she had had the gift of bi-location.

The generation of that dynamism was not without substantial difficulties that sometimes drove some members of her group to the edge of losing faith in the whole idea. Without telling the committee about it, Nick Robinson commissioned, out of his own funds, a private project from the Lansdowne Market Research company in the middle of the summer. It was qualitative research, designed to give him some answers to questions that had been bothering him. He wanted some objective information on how the public perceived the role of the President, how they would respond to the concept of a more active President, and how they viewed the strengths and weaknesses of the only two candidates whose identities were known at the time – Mary, and Brian Lenihan.

He knew at the time he was commissioning this work that at least some of his colleagues on the committee which had been established to run Mary's campaign would object to scarce resources being used in this way – and indeed, when the existence of the research became apparent some time later, it did cause a huge row on the committee. But Nick was not satisfied that he knew everything he needed to know to contribute to the strategic and tactical decisions that were being made every day by the committee. He needed some kind of a bench-mark of his own against which to weigh up the advice that he was getting from different sources.

Advice had started to come in very early. Eoghan Harris was one of the first converts to Mary's cause. He had heard the announcement on April 4th that Mary was likely to be the Labour candidate, and had immediately seen the potential of her campaign. More than that – he believed that he knew the keys to election for her. As a Workers' Party advisor, he had devised the startlingly successful European election campaign for Proinsias De Rossa the previous summer, and was certain that similar techniques would elect Mary Robinson. He spent all that day and all the following day writing a memo to her that ran to ten pages. It was to have a considerable influence on the way she and Nick prepared for the early phases of the campaign, although some of the claims made on his behalf subsequently, suggesting that he exercised a virtual "Svengali" influence over the campaign, were totally inaccurate, and seen by many as demeaning the strong and independent person that Mary Robinson is.

In his memo, he addressed issues of style (like clothes, photographs, language) and substance (like divorce, abortion, the Constitution). He warned her about what newspapers to go for (the *Sunday World*, the *Independent*, the *Press*), and what to avoid (the *Tribune*, the *Irish Times*). Perhaps the most influential paragraph in his memo was this one:

> One of the classic errors of the hard left is not to understand a simple piece of psychology: ordinary people are full of pity, but they hate whiners. So Mary should visit Rape Crisis centres, but stress the positive. She must visit mental hospitals, but where we see things done so well that we don't grudge a call for more cash. She must visit the disabled, but disabled on the move. DON'T RUN A POVERTY CAMPAIGN. RUN A CARING CAMPAIGN.

Mary and Nick understood very well the psychological point he was making, and phrases like "fight-back spirit" became central to her message (the phrase was actually coined by Catherine Donnelly, another media expert who was giving her time voluntarily). But they were afraid that any intervention or advice from Eoghan Harris would be rejected out of hand by their Labour Party sponsors, since Harris had recently resigned from the Workers' Party in a blazing row about the future direction of that party. When Mary Robinson mentioned Harris's approach to John Rogers (without giving him any details), he warned that in his view there was a need for considerable care in any dealings with Harris, particularly having regard to the bitterness between Eoghan and the Workers' Party, at a time when efforts were being made to recruit them to the cause. As a consequence, at least for the time being, Eoghan Harris was kept at arm's length, free to contribute ideas – extraordinarily creative ideas in many cases – but not in a position to exercise the control that he would have wished for. However, he seemed to be happy to go along with that.

The Robinsons were anxious to ensure that Harris's early memo would influence the rest of the campaign team, but unwilling to expose the ideas as his. So they decided to conceal the authorship of his advice – advice which nobody in the campaign was likely to disagree with, if they had known about it, whatever its source.

A two-page document, incorporating Harris's ideas, was drawn up by Nick Robinson, Peter MacMenamin and Bride Rosney and submitted to the campaign committee.

These two events – the secret commissioning of research, and the concealment of Eoghan Harris's paper on approaches to effective communication – were symptomatic of a major problem. In the several weeks after Mary's ratification as the candidate, there had been a great deal of toing and froing between Mary and the various Labour Party people involved, while a structure for dealing with the campaign was being developed. Not all of these contacts had inspired mutual trust. A view was growing among Mary's close personal advisors that the Labour Party was primarily interested in exploiting Mary's candidacy to broaden its own base of support. They did not see the party treating the campaign with the same total urgency and commitment that they felt themselves.

On the other hand, some senior party members at least were beginning to feel that the Robinsons were themselves beginning to look at the party as "nomination fodder", to be jollied along until the formal Oireachtas nomination was secured, but to be kept at a distance, simply because the party was small, and might be offensive to some of the constituency that Mary was hoping to attract. Members of the party involved in the campaign began to notice the efforts that were apparently being made to preserve as much distance as possible between the candidate and the party.

It didn't at that stage occur to anyone to explain that both sides of the equation had a mutual interest. The Labour Party was committed to the view that it had to build a consensus around Mary, even if it meant submerging its own identity for the purpose. But that was never effectively communicated to Mary – at least to the point where she could trust it implicitly. For her part, she was so busy ensuring that no one organisation secured a "proprietorial" interest in her that she never succeeded in reassuring the Labour Party that their efforts would be as fully repaid as it was in her power to deliver.

Eventually, a small committee was established to run the campaign. Chaired by Ruairi Quinn, who was thus handed a task that was to tax all of his diplomatic and negotiating skills, it consisted of Mary's nominees, Mary herself, Nick, Bride Rosney and Peter Mac-Menamin. The Labour Party nominated, in addition to Ruairi Quinn, John Rogers, Fergus Finlay and Ray Kavanagh, General Secretary of the party. At the very first meeting, on the 31st of May, a number of "staff" were seconded to the campaign: Ita McAuliffe, to provide secretarial and administrative back-up to the committee; Anne Byrne, to run individual projects and to build up a talent bank, and Ann Lane, Mary's personal secretary, to take charge of the campaign diary. Fergus Finlay was to co-ordinate and oversee staff efforts as a full member of the committee. (Other staff members were described throughout as being "in attendance" at committee meetings, rather than "present" – a sore point, until the question of the financial deficit came up at the end of the campaign, and someone made the point that "everyone present has a moral responsibility for the deficit". "That means those who were only in attendance are off the hook," one of the staff members pointed out.) With the exception of Ann Lane, all of the personnel resources at that stage were provided by the Labour Party.

It was a committee which consisted of a number of powerful individuals, each of them committed to making a success of Mary's candidacy, and each with their own very strong ideas about how it should be done. The mix was often explosive – but in the end, it was both dynamic and creative. The credit for that ultimately belonged to Ruairi Quinn, who saw his role as that of making a coherent whole out of a lot of disparate elements. Being director of elections was not a new experience for Ruairi – he had steered Barry Desmond's campaign for Europe the previous summer. He was used to dealing with temperament in all its forms, and to welding difficult and talented people together into a team. There were times in the course of this campaign when he despaired of creating a unity of purpose out of the tension around him – as he said himself, "If only I had hair to tear out!" – but ultimately, as things began to fall into place, the confidence that he was backing a winner grew, and as it did, the problems of encouraging strong-willed people to work together diminished.

There was no-one on the committee more strong-willed than Bride Rosney, who had known Mary for twelve years. She had been involved with her during the Wood Quay campaign. Bride's political and organisational experience was gained in that campaign and on other environmental issues, as well as in trade union politics. She was perhaps Mary's closest friend and advisor outside the family. A tough, determined woman, Bride made up her mind from the start that the committee would be run along professional lines. She insisted on minutes, and was always the first to point out any inaccuracies in them.

She made it clear too from the beginning that she was not prepared to tolerate even the slightest doubt being expressed about the inevitability of winning. Some other members of the committee felt that Bride did not regard the Labour Party as the perfect vehicle for Mary's candidacy – she saw the party as not being willing enough to pay the various prices that victory requires – and it was a long time before she began to develop a grudging respect for the party's professionalism and skill. Her early doubts about the party put her in a position where, throughout the campaign, she was involved in conflict with them at national and at local level. Many of the party's deputies, for example, wondered aloud how Bride could be so certain that she appeared to know better than they did how to maximise the vote in their own constituencies. She often appeared to thrive on being at the centre of the storm, and didn't appear to be aware that other members of the committee were spending at least part of their time soothing the tempers she had frayed. Her authority on the committee derived from the fact that Mary was prepared to listen to her at all times, and Bride believed only in exercising that authority to ensure that the job was done according to Mary's specifications.

Peter MacMenamin, on the other hand, said very little at strategy meetings, preferring to express his opinions privately. Although a party member, he was on the committee at Mary's suggestion, and acted at all times as her agent. Formerly elected President of the Teachers' Union of Ireland, of which he is now a fulltime official, he also had experience of general elections with the Labour Party. He saw it as his role to be the one to put forward criticisms that Mary would have been inhibited about – if there was fault to be found with the activities of any member of the campaign team, it was Peter who was more likely to utter it than anyone else. Some members of the team found his often brooding and silent presence unnerving.

John Rogers had been the closest advisor to Dick Spring since the day Spring took up leadership of the party, and for a good many years before that. He had served as Attorney General, and he knew the party, the processes of Government, and the vicissitudes of elections inside out. He also knew Mary very well, since they were both practitioners at the bar together. In fact, in the early days of the campaign, until Mary suspended her law practice, they had been working on a major case together, a case that John eventually finished in the Supreme Court shortly before the election. Rogers, although he is a strong believer in confidentiality, and is temperamentally committed to close counsel, was never unwilling to speak his mind in a very forthright way. He acted very often as a bridge between the party and Mary, and sought from the beginning to forge a better understanding in her of how the party thinks and works, and in the party of what drives Mary.

Ray Kavanagh, General Secretary of the party, knew every branch and every constituency intimately. He knew how to motivate them – and what would turn them off. Although a mild-mannered individual, he is very stubborn, with his own very clear ideas about the pace at which people react to change. As national director of elections in two general election campaigns he would not be the kind of man to take easily to the notion that Bride, or later Brenda O'Hanlon, would know better than he how to run a national organisation.

Fergus Finlay is assistant to Dick Spring and spokesperson for the Labour Party. In common with the other members, he had a role on the committee in the development of strategy, and he was also to maintain contact with the national media, especially the political correspondents for RTE, Century, and the daily papers. Some members of the committee found him abrasive and too inclined to push the party line.

Later in the campaign, Eamon Gilmore of the Workers' Party was co-opted as a full member of the committee, That party had originally opted to run their own campaign and up to the time of Eamon's involvement, liaison had been maintained through regular meetings between Ruairi Quinn and Pat Rabbitte. Eamon saw his role on the committee to contribute ideas in respect of areas where the Workers' Party was strong, particularly the Dublin area, but he was also a useful contributor of ideas about communication generally. By the time he joined the committee, most of the antagonisms and tensions had been ironed out.

For a long time, though, antagonism dominated the work of the committee. From the very first meeting, the atmosphere was tense, and frequently carping. Two camps emerged, the Robinson camp and the Labour camp. The Robinson camp were anxious from an early stage to secure the endorsement of the Workers' Party, the Progressive Democrats, the Green Party and as many other groups as possible, including independent senators and TDs. They suspected the Labour camp of dragging its heels. The Labour camp, on the other hand, were becoming more and more convinced that the Robinson camp was trying to play down its association with Labour all the time. These suspicions festered on both sides for months – but unfortunately, a great deal of time was allowed to lapse before they were properly aired and dealt with.

Mary Robinson had the essential qualities that a great political candidate needs – she had a total belief not only in her ability to win, but also in the fact that if elected, she would make a great President. As a result, she was totally determined to win, and grew quickly impatient with what she perceived as the fact that that determination was not shared to a sufficient extent by the Labour Party people around her. All they wanted, in her view, was for her to put in a good credible performance. Labour would regard 20 per cent of the national vote as a victory for *them* – even if it was a crushing defeat for *her*.

There was some logic in Mary's reasoning. The calculations that had been done on the Labour side did not, in the early days, suggest that a victory for Mary was a major probability. It was described more often as a mathematical possibility – heavily dependent on the quirks of the proportional representation system. And it is true too that many Labour people would have regarded 20 per cent of the vote as a victory.

But there was another side to it. Most of the party people directly involved in the campaign had aggregated many years of experience in running national campaigns. They had never undertaken a six-month campaign, but were nevertheless conscious – more conscious, they felt, than Mary was – of the need for proper pacing and build-up. They were acutely aware, too, of the scarce resources at their disposal.

There was a difference too in the tactical approach adopted to some of the media. Several of the rows in the early days of the campaign centred on newspaper interviews that had been given by party people which failed to describe Mary as the certain winner of the election. These interviews, in Mary's eyes and in the eyes of the people around her, especially Peter MacMenamin, were too downbeat and unlikely to inspire.

Party people had a different perspective. Not one political reporter in those days gave Mary a chance of winning – they all agreed it was a good idea that she should run, and that she was capable of mounting a good campaign, full of ideas and energy. But winning against the big battalions? It flew too much in the face of conventional wisdom to be even conceivable.

So the task, as the party people saw it, was to persuade the media, painstakingly and gradually, that Mary could come second, and after that, who knows? Every previous example of a three-cornered race under proportional representation was examined and demonstrated, and one simple fact emerged: when there are three candidates in a proportional representation election in Ireland, the voters divide into Fianna Fáil and anti-Fianna Fáil. As a result, the candidate who comes second on the first count wins on transfers as often as not. The use of this logic was a lot less inspirational than talking about Mary's magical appeal, but it was gradually conveying the impression that Mary could win, and in the eyes of some members of the committee, that was more credible than asserting that she was bound to win.

Others felt that approaching the problem that way was tantamount to an admission that she was more likely to lose in the end.

But "the night of the brown rose" was the first time that the tensions in the group surfaced in a significant way. Artwork for a campaign logo had been commissioned by Ruairi Quinn from the advertising agency, Quinn McDonnell Pattison, and was made available for a committee meeting on June 13th. But Nick Robinson had also commissioned artwork from a designer working freelance, Carol Coffey, and brought that along, together with a very insistent recommendation that it be adopted. Both concepts incorporated a rose, as had been agreed (it was considered an important symbol of a broad left campaign), but the rose that Nick produced was brown – or, in his description, "terracotta".

It was agreed to adopt Nick's rose – provided it was red. But the meeting quickly divided over the issue of the colour of the rose, and a bitter argument ensued. Terracotta it must be, one side argued. Nothing is acceptable but red, said the other. Accusations began to be hurled, with one side being accused of ignoring the need for subtlety in design, and the other being accused of wanting to move away from meaningful association with the left. Voices were never raised, but a chill entered the atmosphere that it took several weeks to dispel. It took all of Ruairi Quinn's tact to ensure that relations between the two sides remained civilised enough for work to continue, and in the end a graceful concession by Nick on the colour of the rose saved the day.

When issues of that sort predominate discussion, it can only be because something has got way out of proportion. In this case it was a lack of trust – trust on the part of the candidate that the party was really up to the job, and meant to honour its commitments to the fullest; and trust on the part of the party that the candidate was committed to being a left-wing champion in the first place. For a while, both sides operated together only because they knew they were stuck with one another, and because the credibility of each side would be fatally damaged if there were any public differences.

But in the kind of atmosphere that had been generated – and that nobody for months tried to confront – blame became a feature of many of the meetings. Mary had prepared a thoughtful speech for the launch of a book about disabled people in June, but no media turned up. Bride had stood watching the "Metrovision" board in O'Connell Street for fifteen minutes, to see a message about Mary that was supposed to appear every six minutes. Mary had attended the Xtravision World Cup Video show in the RDS, and the organisation of the event was chaotic. For a long time it seemed to many members of the committee that they could do nothing right.

At times the problems of communication reached farcical levels. One of the committee staff, Anne Byrne, was delegated the job of preparing the press launch of the committee's new headquarters, which had been donated by the Manufacturing, Science, Finance (MSF) Union in the basement of 15 Merrion Square. The occasion was to involve not only media people, but a number of invited personalities who were prepared to lend their names to the occasion. As a consequence, it was agreed to serve a light lunch, and Anne contacted the Larkin Unemployed Centre and asked them to do the catering. As she normally would when organising such an event, she drew up a detailed checklist to ensure that nothing was overlooked. Nick asked for a copy, and after studying it carefully advised Anne that she had apparently overlooked the need to provide cutlery for the food. On the morning of the launch itself, she got a phone call from the Robinson household saying that when the ladies toilet had been checked three days earlier, there had been no toilet paper, and if she wished, they would deliver some to her in the course of the morning!

The problems of communication and trust were accentuated in the early days by a sense of drift. It was hard to interest the media in the fact that a presidential campaign was under way – particularly hard because there was still only one candidate in the race. And early opinion poll information was either discouraging or inconclusive to the point of being meaningless. An Irish Marketing Surveys poll in June gave Mary 9 per cent – the same figure as Noel Browne, who had by then been eliminated as a candidate, and two points behind Carmencita Hederman. A poll conducted for the *Sunday Business*

Post was slightly more encouraging. In the hypothetical situation of a three-way contest between Garret FitzGerald, Brian Lenihan, and Mary, it showed Mary coming third, but with 18 per cent of the vote. If the three candidates were FitzGerald, Haughey and Robinson, the poll showed Mary's figures climbing to 23 per cent.

This information did little more than confirm that the strategy behind Mary's selection was basically correct – that Mary would attract a personal vote well in excess of the party that nominated her. And with no campaign yet under way, and no real time to establish a national profile for Mary, the baseline figures of 18-23 per cent gave some grounds for hope.

There was even more ground for optimism available in Fine Gael's difficulties in finding a candidate. Members of Mary's committee had been certain for months that Garret FitzGerald would not be a candidate, and believed it highly unlikely that Peter Barry would be willing to run. Information given to some members of the committee by a Fine Gael source in the late summer convinced them that Fine Gael were in deep trouble.

The largest opposition Party had been promised by its leader Alan Dukes, at its Árd Fheis in February, that Fine Gael would be contesting the presidency seriously, with a candidate of vigour and substance. Although many delegates believed he had Garret FitzGerald in mind, he had already begun the search for an alternative at that stage. As part of this process, one of the market research companies had been commissioned to establish the major qualifications in a candidate, and to measure selected names against those qualifications. This work was to be undertaken privately, but a copy of the results was seen by some of Mary Robinson's committee.

It revealed that three candidates were still under consideration by Fine Gael – Peter Barry, Avril Doyle and Austin Currie. Under the various headings identified as important – experience, national profile, appeal, integrity, etc. – Peter Barry scored best, with Avril Doyle a poor second, and Austin Currie in a dismal third place. On the basis of this data, Fine Gael, who couldn't have Garret FitzGerald, would have to try to persuade Peter Barry to run. Otherwise, if they picked Avril Doyle, they would face the accusation that they were trying to run a "copy cat" candidate – as one member of the committee put it, a "haute couture version of Mary Robinson". The only thing the committee could be reasonably confident of was that Fine Gael, on the basis of the data available to it, was unlikely to go for Austin Currie!

There was little enough in all of this for the committee to get its teeth into. That was one of the reasons why Nick had decided to commission the research referred to earlier. It yielded some interesting information – such as the fact that most people were disgruntled with the role played by President Hillery, but unwilling to see the Constitution tampered with to make the role more meaningful. The message that was coming across was that if a campaign for a more active role for the presidency, within the existing constitutional parameters, could be effectively sold, people would be more likely to vote for the candidate who best suited the revised job specification.

Secondly, the presidency was not perceived as giving value for money. The candidate who made a value-for-money presidency a central policy plank would be likely to evoke a good response.

But would that candidate be Mary? At the time the research was undertaken, Austin Currie had still not emerged, and Brian Lenihan was the likely, though still unofficial, Fianna Fáil candidate. The perception of Mary that emerged from the research showed that there was a lot of work to be done on how she got her message, and herself, across. She was perceived as aloof, intimidating, too feminist, a lawyer (ugh!), and privileged. There was a great deal of confusion among the people surveyed as to her religion.

On the positive side, there was some consensus that a woman would break the mould, and bring feminine qualities of compassion and concern to the office. She was also seen as considerably more attractive than Brian Lenihan!

Nick assimilated this information quietly, and incorporated a lot of it into the decision-making process. For example, when discussion took place about the need to soften and round off Mary's image, with hair and clothes changes, Nick was the one most forceful in his encouragement. As it happened, Mary needed little persuasion in this regard. She saw herself from the start as applying for a job – the most important job she had ever applied for – and accepted readily that grooming was a vital part of the process. Catherine Donnelly recommended a hair stylist – and a range of fashion designers, and Brenda O'Hanlon organised a number of fittings.

Brenda had "come aboard" at the start of August. She was a senior public relations executive with a large network of media contacts and a reputation second to none in her field. Apart from some voluntary work for David Norris she had no previous political experience. Prior to August, she had attended a number of meetings of a "media committee" that had been established, to try to attract as many ideas as possible from people who were volunteering to help – Catherine Donnelly, Colm Ó Briain, and others. One of the discoveries made at this time was that there was an enormous fund of goodwill towards Mary's candidacy from people in the advertising and media world, but many of them were very constrained, either because their agencies frowned on political involvement or were already committed to other parties. To overcome this problem, several members of the committee, especially Nick, met a number of people privately, on a one-to-one basis, to get ideas from them without revealing their identities.

Catherine Donnelly in particular was a seemingly endless fund of ideas and information. Asked to produce a range of possible slogans, she came up within hours with a list which included the following:

"Mary Robinson. If you're old enough to vote, and young enough to care."

"Politicians debate issues. Presidents address them."

"Some issues are too small for politicians. Or too big."

"Vote for a working President. There are enough monuments in the Park."

"The Presidency is not a reward. It's a challenge."

"An office is a place of work. Not retirement."

Each of these was seen as addressing particular aspects of the campaign. The one that encompassed everything that Mary was trying to present was "A President with a Purpose". Up to then, the campaign had been working with Eoghan Harris's suggested slogan (which most committee members thought had come from Nick) of "A President for all the People". Catherine's was adopted the moment it was produced – one of the rare occasions up to then that the committee was in total unanimity.

Brenda O'Hanlon was one of the people who was constrained by the attitude of her employers, the Wilson Hartnell public relations agency, which stayed clear of political involvements as a matter of policy. Brenda herself had been personally committed to the notion of a Robinson presidency from the moment it had been announced as a possibility. Mary liked her, and admired her emphasis on delivery – she believed in getting the job done, no matter how big or small it was. She was also very upbeat, convinced from the start that Mary couldn't fail.

But there was a problem. Mary was convinced that the new headquarters needed someone to run it full-time, and that the person should be Brenda. Wilson Hartnell would have had difficulty in allowing Brenda to take time off, because it would associate them with the campaign. Besides, money wasn't coming in fast enough to warrant employing a full-time professional. Mary solved this problem herself, by offering Brenda a contract which would be paid for out of Mary's own resources. It took Brenda less than an hour to think about it, and hand in her notice to her employers.

With a hard-driving person in charge in headquarters, and additional secretarial back-up (in addition to Ita McAuliffe, the Labour Party donated one of its head-office staff, Angie Mulroy, to work full time in the headquarters), things slowly began to fall into place. There were frequent rows, of course. Brenda was not used to working in situations where the budget was very tight and the staff almost entirely voluntary. Tact was not Brenda's strong point – she neither suffered fools gladly nor was ever prepared to take No for an answer, and was frequently, as a result, at the eye of a hurricane. On one occasion, Mary herself had to mediate in a row between Brenda and Angie Mulroy, as they were finding it increasingly difficult to work together. Angie, who had come from party head office, was highly regarded by party members, and a public row would have had wider repercussions in the committee as a whole. Fortunately, both individuals managed to subsume their antagonism to one another in the one thing they had in common – their admiration for Mary.

A fund-raising committee was established under Niall Greene, a senior executive with Guinness Peat Aviation who had been a long-term member of the Labour Party, and Greg Sparks, also a Labour Party member and a partner in the accountancy firm of Farrell, Grant and Sparks. The first fund-raising venture – a series of newspaper advertisements under the slogan " Put your hand in your pocket for a President who isn't in anybody's" was less than successful. But now a more systematic approach began to take shape. This was helped very considerably by a number of people with experience of the business world, notably Carton Finnegan and Kevin Bourke, both unpaid volunteers, who prepared lists of businesses and professional groups that could be approached, and put together small and very hard-working teams of yet more volunteers to send out mail shots and carry on the often thankless task of ringing businesses to implore them for donations.

As a result, money started to come in steadily, though never in large enough quantities. Business had opted out of this election, largely on the basis that it was not an election that would decide any issues of executive power. Company after company told the fund-raisers that "If this were a general election, there'd be no problem – because then it would be in our interests to contribute ..." More than one of the people involved began to wonder what were the factors that encouraged business to contribute to politics in the normal way. If there had to be something in it for them, what was the something?

But despite that, there were clear signs in the financial response the committee was getting that something big was beginning to happen. It wasn't so much in the amount of money, but rather in the type of money that was coming in. People who in the normal way simply cannot afford to contribute to political campaigns – pensioners, unemployed people, widows – sent in pounds and fivers. Over the entire campaign, the average contribution never got much bigger than twenty pounds, but they were coming from every corner of the country – from Donegal, the Aran Islands, Kerry, the North of Ireland – and from young and old alike. Analysing the sources of the money became a much more encouraging exercise than counting it.

In headquarters too, there were signs of increasing action. Volunteers were pouring in, sometimes as many as seventy a week. There was no doubt that Mary Robinson's appeal was widespread. People were willing to do anything – canvass their own street, stuff envelopes, make tea for any canvassers who wanted to call. People who in some cases had difficulty getting up and down the steep steps that led to the basement in 15 Merrion Square would still make the trip every day to help. Some became permanent, full-time, (and still unpaid) members of the team. Aoife Breslin, John Gogan, Angela Douglas, Vincent Quinn – as time went on the numbers grew, and there were days when Brenda found it difficult to find work for all the people who were willing to help. All were to become invaluable members of an extraordinarily dedicated team, surviving rows and screaming matches, to see a dream fulfilled.

In Leinster House, too, machinery was beginning to click into gear. Christy Kelly, the Labour Party printer, cleared his desk and for six weeks printed nothing but the same leaflet, a small A5 leaflet on cheap paper that featured Mary's photograph and a simple message. By the end of it, he had produced nearly two million copies of the same leaflet, and could recite the message by heart. When he was finished, he immediately began work on a polling-day card, to be handed out outside polling stations on November 7th, with the last-minute message, "Vote No.1 Mary Robinson". A half-million were produced in all, by one printer working ten hours a day on an outdated offset litho machine that miraculously, never broke down once!

Despite the increasing pace of activity and organisation, tension continued to fester within the committee. Early in October there was a row about a statement that had been drafted by Eoghan Harris, and issued without consultation, which accused Brian Lenihan of lacking "street cred" and compared him to "an ageing movie queen" for refusing to participate in debates with the other candidates.

But it was the revelation about Nick's private research that brought the whole situation to a head, and finally cleared the air. It had been agreed that with the campaign moving towards its final phase, a core management group would meet every morning in campaign headquarters at 8.00 a.m. This group was to consist of Nick, Brenda, Bride, Ray Kavanagh, and Fergus Finlay, meeting under Ruairi Quinn's chairmanship.

It was at one of the very earliest of these daily meetings that the market research came up. The bill from Lansdowne, which had been supposed to go directly to Nick, came instead to the committee. Members who had not known about it were outraged – not because of the cost, since Nick confirmed that he would be meeting that himself – but because it was a clear indication of a complete lack of trust. Nick was accused directly at the meeting of deliberately trying to keep members of the committee in the dark.

The result was an extremely healthy discussion, which should have taken place months earlier. Nick outlined his position, and he was supported by Bride. They had thrown themselves headlong into the campaign, he said, and from the very first week he and Mary had spent long hours travelling the country, as had been agreed. But for a lot of the time they felt they were entirely alone – inadequate arrangements had been made to receive them locally, fundraising had been slow to get off the ground. In general terms they felt that the party was not treating their efforts with the urgency that they deserved, and the result was that they had felt isolated, and compelled to turn for advice and guidance wherever they could get it. The situation had improved from September on, but up to then they felt let down by the party that had asked them to run in the first place.

This came as a shock to the party people present, who had for months harboured the conviction that the Robinsons wanted to keep their distance from the party, in the belief that association would damage their chances. Examples of this were pointed out in the discussion, and for the first time since the campaign started, each "camp" aired its fears and resentments for the benefit of the other.

At the end, there was general agreement among the group that secrecy was intensely damaging and would have to be avoided. From that moment on, resentment was put to one side. One of the remarkable features of the entire set of feelings that existed within the organisation was that it had never surfaced in public, or infected other levels of the campaign – if it had, it would have caused irreparable damage. It was perhaps the best measure of the commitment of everybody involved to Mary Robinson that personal feelings, which often ran high, were never once allowed to get in the way of the ultimate objective of winning the presidency for her.

It would perhaps be overstating the case to say that after the row had finally exploded, everyone on the committee became firm friends. There continued to be disagreements and rows right up to the end – but now they were conducted from a different perspective. Gradually, a degree of respect had built up among the different members of the committee for each other. They mightn't necessarily like each other or each other's methods, but each member recognised the total commitment of the others to the overall objective and the fact that everyone was applying their own brand of professional expertise.

It made the job easier, and the objective all the more worthwhile.

"Mná na hÉireann!"

Nick Robinson had a very simple motivation for wanting to see Mary elected as President of Ireland. He loves his wife, and he believes that there is no-one who can bring more quality to bear on the office than she can. That was the reason he threw himself so whole-heartedly into the campaign to elect her, and why he was prepared to put up with the privations of a long and wearisome campaign for her sake.

It certainly wasn't for his own sake. Although not a public man, he is successful in his own right, with his own circle of friends and interests. He knew from the start that the campaign would involve him in as much grinding physical activity as it would Mary, and he's a man who relishes putting his feet up as much as anyone else. He knew too that it would involve his portrayal in a somewhat subservient position, although theirs had always been a marriage based on total equality. He resigned himself to that right at the beginning.

That's not to say that he is a man without ego – on the contrary, he's very aware of his own worth. In the end though, the lack of insecurity that comes from his degree of self-confidence made it easier for him to support Mary from the first row in the audience, rather than from centre stage.

At the end of October, Nick was ill. He and Mary had taken the tour bus from Kerry into Cork city, and had arrived to find the city in the grip of the jazz festival. Nick had been nursing a heavy cold for days, and the Kerry rain had turned it into a severe bronchial infection. Mary was worried about him, and asked Pat Magner, who was organising their visit to Cork, to get a doctor.

But getting a doctor to the Metropole Hotel on a bank holiday Monday in the middle of the jazz festival is not easy, especially as Magner had been asked to be discreet – the last thing anyone needed at that stage was a rumour that Mary Robinson, rather than Brian

Lenihan, was in a doctor's care. By the time a doctor arrived in the hotel, Mary had had to leave, to go to the RTE studios in Union Quay, where she was doing an important link-up for a live interview on the BBC's Woman's Hour. And Nick, despite feeling awful, had insisted on going with her.

He knew that Mary derived considerable reassurance from having him in eye contact when she was doing a major interview – if not actually in the studio, then where she could see him through a glass panel in the control room. It helped her to pace herself, and to have a sense of always talking to someone on a one-to-one basis, which was particularly important if the interview was with a disembodied voice down the line.

By the time the doctor's car had been guided through the packed streets by a motorcycle policeman to RTE, Nick was nearly purple in the face from trying not to cough in the studio. He said afterwards that if he had remembered it was the BBC he would never have gone into the studio – at least on RTE you could cough during the commercials! The doctor waited patiently until the programme was over, and then injected Nick with antibiotics.

Throughout all that tour, Nick seldom left his wife's side. At the same time he acted as constant liaison with the committee in Dublin, assimilating information, making decisions, suggesting directions. He never allowed himself to look or sound tired – and he made it his business to ensure that Mary got enough rest and food. Whenever something needed to be done first, and apologised for afterwards, as often happens in political campaigns – one campaign stop too many that has to be cancelled, a deputation that just can't be seen – it was Nick who did it. In short, he acted as husband and agent, guardian and moral support from start to finish.

It was an unusual role for a man in Irish politics – but this was to be, for the first time in Irish politics, a women's campaign, with men increasingly in a supportive position. That was not the way it was planned – in fact, a number of the strategists involved in preparing for the campaign doubted seriously if there was a woman's vote in the election. Experience had suggested that no matter what the issue, women just as much as men voted along party lines. And there was a degree of empirical evidence to back up this assumption.

To take one example, one recent election had been studied – the 1987 general election result in the Dublin South constituency, which covers a largely middle class area, and has elected its fair share of liberal personalities. The 1987 result was instructive, because it featured three prominent women – Nuala Fennell, Anne Colley, and Eithne Fitzgerald – who at different stages of the count were in a position to transfer votes to one another. If they had done so, the constituency could well have returned two women in that election. But there was no significant transfer between the women candidates, and only one of them was elected as a result.

Those less interested in statistics and more in image, like Eoghan Harris, failed to spot the direct impact on women of Mary's candidacy too. Harris's original memo stressed that Mary should aim to come across as:

The kind of competent, compassionate, caring and attractive woman we would like our wife/daughter/sister/mother/girlfriend to be if we are men; and the kind of woman we want to be if we are women – and remember women's images of the ideal are also reflections of how men view that ideal too. For women, Mary should be the kind of woman they want to be; for men, the kind of woman they would like to be seen with in public, or to talk with in private.

Mary Robinson's election was different, and unique. Many thousands of women decided that they didn't want to be "reflections of how men view the ideal". They voted for Mary as women in their own right, and many hundreds more worked for her. Without the women who worked for her and supported her, she would have lost the election by a significant margin. In the campaigns run by the other parties, the evidence of Mary's impact on women was clear. Fianna Fáil knew long before November 7th that they had lost a lot of women to Mary Robinson – and made a number of feeble efforts to convince the public that both Brian Lenihan and Charles J Haughey had spent a lifetime each in politics to further the cause of women.

Fine Gael were even more acutely aware of the number of women who had committed themselves to Mary Robinson. Shortly before the close of nominations, a number of Fine Gael front benchers even gave some consideration to the idea of nominating Carmencita Hederman, as well as Austin Currie, with a view to neutralising the impact that Mary was making among women voters. They abandoned the idea only when one of them remarked "how would it look if we allowed Carmencita into the race and she ended up beating Austin Currie into *fourth* place?"

But by the time the other parties realised the strategic role being played by women, it was too late. Hundreds of women all over Ireland – from Kay McGlinchey in Donegal to Mary O'Shea in Cork – women who had no party political axes to grind, had already emerged into key roles in the dozens of local campaigns that were run on Mary's behalf. The experiences of just a few of them, of widely differing ages and backgrounds, may serve to illustrate the role that women played in ensuring that by the end, Mary's victory was going to be clearly visible as a triumph almost of a personal kind for women everywhere.

Long before that, the Robinson campaign had opened its headquarters in the basement of 15 Merrion Square. One of the very first people to climb down the iron stairs to the office was an elderly woman who said she had admired Mary for a long time, and was prepared to do anything she could to help. The feeling in the office was that it was unfair to ask someone who was obviously getting on in years to stump the streets canvassing. Fortunately there was a mail shot to be got out – envelopes to be stuffed and licked. For days Brigid Murphy – that was her name – worked industriously, chatting with the younger workers who were coming and going.

Over coffee one morning, the talk turned to Áras an Uachtaráin. Nobody there had ever seen the inside of the Áras, and there was a great deal of curiosity about what it was like.

"I can tell you about it," said Brigid, "I used to work there."

It transpired that fifty-one years earlier, Brigid had retired from

Áras an Uachtaráin – because she had got married. Before that, she had been Secretary to Douglas Hyde, the first President of Ireland. At the time she worked in the Áras, every member of staff spoke Irish fluently – except the butler, because it had been impossible to procure an Irish-speaking butler!

Brigid had never taken part in a political campaign in her life until the day she heard that Mary Robinson was going to be a candidate for the Park. The moment she heard the news, she concluded that nothing could be more fitting than that a woman of Mary's education and culture should be in the Park.

Brigid still maintains stoutly that she committed herself to Mary Robinson as the best candidate for the job -- and not because she was a woman. But it had taken something special to draw Brigid into that decision to go to Merrion Square in July, and to spend the next few months working as hard as she ever had in her more than seventy years. Licking and stuffing envelopes is not sustaining work for someone as active and determined as Brigid, and before long she was out on the streets, going from door to door in Terenure and Rathmines, and building up her own network of Mary Robinson supporters.

She made friends on the campaign trail – people like Eithne Flanagan, a retired solicitor who had worked in the fifties on behalf of Clann na Poblachta. Eithne and Brigid were both anxious to go to Ballina for the start of the national tour in October, but shortly before that, Eithne had a bad fall, which left her with a badly bruised face. Nothing daunted, they went anyway, and many members of the campaign marvelled at their stamina and dedication. Watching them march up the main street in Castlebar on the evening of first day of the national tour, both erect and proud, was an inspiration to younger members of the team already beginning to flag.

Neither Eithne nor Brigid would describe themselves as classical feminists, but simply as women who said "Why not?" Why should a bright and capable woman be deemed unsuitable for a job, just because she was a woman? Hadn't Mary Robinson proved that she had the credentials and the track record to show that she could hold her head up with the very best?

Darina and Myrtle Allen felt much the same way. Mary had written to them – and to a lot of other well-known people – right at the start of the campaign, looking for support. They were among the first to offer help, and were unstinting in their efforts. Neither had ever been involved in politics before. Darina Allen readily admits that she doesn't vote for political parties, but for individuals. She saw Mary Robinson as a classic patriot, a woman who would work for, and represent, Ireland with distinction. As Darina put it herself, "How could you refuse to work for someone that you'd be proud – as an Irishwoman – to see representing you?"

They had never worked for an individual before, and had no experience of campaigns or campaigning. But this time they were prepared to work – and to spend – for a person that neither of them had ever met. There was a number of things they could do. They lent their names to Mary, and agreed to appear in public with her at every opportunity, knowing that they would be used for publicity purposes for the campaign. They hosted receptions for her, arranging the guest lists and organising all the catering – the first one, in the Crawford Gallery in Cork, attracted over two hundred people and provided an invaluable opportunity for Mary to put down roots in the city in the early days. They could establish networks of friends and colleagues prepared to help.

And they did all that and more. Women who were successful in their own right added credibility and lustre to Mary's campaign. They made it possible to portray Mary as a winner very early on. And the women who did that did so at some risk to their own reputations. Nobody wants to be associated with a loser, or with a cause that is going nowhere. But the commitment of the Allens and others was total. On polling day itself, Darina Allen was running one of her successful schools in Ballymaloe. She had over forty students, all of them (by then) committed to voting for Mary, but none in a position to do so, because they were all away from home. Darina agonised long and hard about whether she should send them all home – her own husband had been dispatched to spend his day driving people to and from the local polling station – and in the end decided that any

*A future President with a future President – Senator Mary Robinson
hands Minister for Foreign Affairs, Dr Patrick Hillery, the Videl
Report, May 1972. (Photo courtesy Irish Press)*

Youthful vigour – already a Senator and Professor of Law by the age of 25, Mary is re-elected to the Senate at Trinity aged 29, May 1973. (Independent Newspapers)

Mansion House Dublin, October 1974. The Anti-Internment Rally was supported by many household names, including Charles Haughey and Austin Currie. Here actress Siobhán McKenna (left) joins Senator Mary Robinson. (Irish Press)

Above: Outside Dáil Éireann, September 1978. The campaign to save the archaeological site at Wood Quay involved thousands of supporters. Mary addresses the protesters before they march to Christchurch. (Irish Times)

Below: Holles Street Hospital, May 1981. Aubrey, the youngest of Nick and Mary's three children, is born. (Irish Times)

*A musical medley – Mary at the launch of Anti-Amendment Music
with musicians Paul Brady (left) and Rocky de Valera (right),
September 1982. (Independent Newspapers)*

A Senator once again – Mary thanks her supporters after being re-elected to the Senate in January 1983. (Independent Newspapers)

*Above: Leinster House Dublin, 19 November 1985. Mary with
Nick after she had resigned from the Labour Party over the
Anglo-Irish Agreement. (Irish Press)*
*Below: Mayo Person of the Year 1988 is – Mary Robinson. Mary
with her father, Dr. Aubrey Bourke (left), and Nick (right).
(Western People)*

*Mary Robinson, Senior Counsel, in full court gear outside
the Four Courts, 1989. (Nick Robinson)*

Leinster House, 24 April 1990. Dick Spring, leader of the Labour Party, announces that Mary has agreed to seek the Labour Party nomination for the presidency. (Irish Times)

Above: Allihies, Co. Cork, 30 April 1990. First official port of call for
the Robinson campaign – at this stage Mary was the only candidate.
(Finn Gillespie)
Below: Mary and Nick at the prehistoric site at Loughcrew,
Co. Meath, May 1990. (Declan Geraghty)

Flying high, Mary visits Inishbofin, Inishturk and Clare Islands,
August 1990. (Western People)

Back down to earth – Mary on foot with islanders on Inishmore,
Co. Galway, August 1990. (Irish Times)

Not quite walking on water – Mary receives a warm welcome on the Inishbofin ferry, August 1990. (Western People)

*A bugler's blessing heralds the arrival of the presidential candidate
to Inishbofin, August 1990. (Western People)*

Brigid Murphy, secretary to Ireland's first President, Douglas Hyde, is first to volunteer as a Mary Robinson campaign worker. (Irish Times)

A determined campaigner gets the point across, September 1990.
(Irish Times)

Presidential hopefuls – from left to right, Brian Lenihan, Mary Robinson and Austin Currie together for the first time at the RTE Radio Centre. (Independent Newspapers)

An urgent message on the campaign trail – Darndale Estate, North County Dublin, October 1990. (Irish Press)

Looking positively presidential – Nick relaxes at home, October 1990.
(Irish Times)

Custom House Dublin, 13 October 1990. From left to right, William, Tessa, Aubrey, Mary and Labour leader Dick Spring after the handing in of the nomination papers. (Irish Press)

Tense but smiling - the presidential runners before the nation on The Late, Late Show. From left to right, Austin and Anita Currie, Mary and Nick, Brian and Ann Lenihan and of course Gay Byrne, 2 November 1990. (Irish Press)

The ups and downs of campaigning – Mary with Nick and supporters in The Square, Tallaght, Dublin, 5 November 1990. (Irish Times)

Four members of the 'Kitchen Cabinet' at their headquarters in Merrion Square: Ruairi Quinn TD, Director of Elections; Bride Rosney, one of the key strategists and long-time friend of Mary and Nick; Brenda O'Hanlon, largely responsible for the media campaign; Fergus Finlay, a close advisor to Dick Spring. (Irish Times)

A touch of parental pride – Mary with her father on the last day of the campaign, 6 November 1990. (Irish Times)

The very last call – Mary visits the Aer Rianta crèche in Dublin Airport, 6 November 1990. (Independent Newspapers)

*Out for the count – Aubrey begins to tire but Mary still looks radiant
at the final count, 9 November 1990. (Irish Press)*

The excitement of the night – a supporter embraces Mary at the RDS,
9 November 1990. (Irish Times)

Victory – Ireland's first female President is elected.
(Independent Newspapers)

Congratulations, Mrs President! – Brian Lenihan (right) offers his felicitations to the new President as Dick Spring, Labour leader, looks on, 9 November 1990. (Irish Times)

Jury's Hotel Dublin, 9 November 1990. International interest in the presidential elections was huge. Members of the international and national press attend a conference immediately following Mary's declaration as President elect of Ireland. (Irish Press)

*And later that night it's party-time for hundreds of campaign workers –
after all their hard work. Here we see Ruairi Quinn, campaign manager,
Mary Robinson and Dick Spring at the Olympic Ballroom, Dublin.
(Independent Newspapers)*

The victor returns home – Mary arrives in her native town, Ballina, Co. Mayo, 11 November 1990. (Irish Press)

A rapturous reception from Mary's extended family in Ballina, Co. Mayo. Back Row (from left): Elizabeth Bourke, Tessa Robinson, Fiona Kerins, Mark Bourke, James Bourke. Centre Row: Frank Kerins, Pamela (Bourke) Kerins, Catherine Bourke, Nick Robinson with son Aubrey, Mary Robinson, Dr. Aubrey Bourke, Ruth Bourke, Adrian Bourke. Front Row: Charles Bourke, Rebecca Bourke, Rickard Bourke, Jane Bourke, Simon Bourke, Robert Bourke (Western People)

publicity attaching to such a move might be counter-productive. As she says now, "If Mary had lost by thirty-nine votes, I'd never have forgiven myself!"

With Sinead Fleming, working for Mary had started as a professional job. She was an employee of a city centre hairdressing salon. Alan Bruton, the proprietor, had advised Mary from early in the campaign about her hair, and had consulted with others about make-up and clothes. When it was obvious that Mary was going to be on the road for the last four weeks of the campaign, and that she would need someone to look after those aspects of her wardrobe, Alan had dispatched several of his staff to work with her in preparation for individual events. Sinead and Mary had hit it off immediately, and Alan agreed to allow her to travel with Mary for the last three weeks.

Sinead is nineteen, with no experience of politics. As a hair stylist, she had to undergo crash courses in make-up and in looking after clothes. And then, for four weeks, she served as Mary's "mirror" ensuring that the candidate never looked anything less than her best, no matter how tired or fed up she might have felt. It was a job that required Sinead to be the first up every morning, and very often the last to go to bed at night. It required her too, occasionally, to pluck up all her courage and order Mary to her room to have her make-up repaired, when Mary was already under pressure on a host of other fronts. Older members of the campaign team who would have broken out in a cold sweat at the thought of ordering Mary around were full of admiration for Sinead's professionalism.

But it was more than professionalism, or a job well done. Sinead hadn't known Mary, or very much about her, when she started to work for her first. If anything, the only feeling she had was awe at her many achievements in the past. But they became fast friends, and confidantes in a way that is not open to many. Sinead had never met anyone with such a wide breadth of knowledge, or so much commitment to causes, or so much determination. For her part, she helped to keep Mary in touch with the energy and enthusiasm of young people. The fact that Sinead was always there when she was needed, never complaining at the lateness (or the earliness) of the hour, and that everything she did was handled with precision and care, was itself a revelation to Mary, who remembered in the process that you don't need letters after your name, or twenty years' experience, to be a consummate professional at what you do.

Sinead and Aoife Breslin became firm friends on that journey around Ireland. Aoife was a grand-daughter of young Jim Larkin, and had left-wing politics in her blood. At twenty-two, she had already been active for several years in Labour Youth, learning how to be a thorn in the side of the party establishment. It had been a disappointment to her when the party had decided to go outside its own ranks for a candidate, and when she was asked to travel around Ireland with Mary on the bus as a general assistant, she agreed to go for the sake of the party – and four weeks later she was totally committed to Mary Robinson the person. In that four weeks, she had seen another side to her – the caring, considerate side, the side that ensured that all the staff were being fed properly, and that no-one was feeling left out or lonely. On one campaign stop, Sinead and Aoife had to go to Mary's hotel room to ensure that her clothes were ready for the next day. There was only a short time available before the bus left to go campaigning for the evening, and the two girls resigned themselves to missing an evening meal. They came downstairs a half-hour later, job done, to discover that Mary had ordered them a meal and was keeping two places for them beside her.

The day that Mary was declared elected, Aoife was asked to present her with flowers. The hug they exchanged on the platform that day was the genuine hug of two close friends. They might have had little in common in terms of age or background, but they liked each other, and that was that.

Aoife also got to know the humorous side of Mary, a side not often enough seen. One of the running jokes on the tour bus was the number of mobile phones that had been acquired. They became almost like children's soothers – there would be panic if a mobile phone wasn't instantly available whenever it was required. People were forever asking each other for the loan of a phone, or for a battery pack, as the phones were constantly running out of power. The men on the bus were particularly addicted, and it quickly became apparent that a mobile phone was a fairly macho symbol of involvement.

Aoife was assigned the job, among dozens of others, of ensuring that the phones were always in working order. It was Mary who led the laughter when one night, as the entire group were gathered for a late supper, Aoife came in and brightly enquired if "any of the men need their batteries recharged before I go to bed?"

Those women who got close to Mary in the course of the campaign came to appreciate a range of personal qualities on top of the track record and the reputation. But thousands of others felt just as close by the time it was all over, and felt a sense of personal investment in her success that is unparalleled in modern Irish politics. For someone who had been on the losing side in the two most recent battles of concern to women, the right to life and the divorce referenda, and who had never chosen to portray herself as a feminist first and foremost, this was a remarkable achievement.

One feminist journalist, Mary Maher, wrote of Mary eight years before her election:

> Away back in 1969, when young Mary Bourke first came on the scene, a lot of newly baptised feminists were disappointed that she wouldn't espouse the women's movement ideology whole-heartedly. She then proceeded to champion every case from women on juries through contraception, divorce, abolition of illegitimacy, equal pay and pensions; and today, she's in court on equity in the social welfare code. No one has shouted less and achieved more.

Perhaps that was the key to it. Mary is a woman who has a deep personal, emotional and intellectual commitment to equality and justice – not alone for other women, but for everybody. She is also a mother, with three young and lively children. She has roots in rural Ireland just as much as in the cities – those who dismissed her as "Dublin 4" would have been astonished to see the rapport between her and the people of the west of Ireland. She does not allow labels to cling to her, although she readily acknowledges a constant set of values. She shouts less, and achieves more.

She is, for those reasons, a woman other women can support – not "the woman they would want to be", but the woman they already are. Women found expression in Mary Robinson, not some kind of vicarious identity. In electing her, they were making their own statement – a statement that things had better be different from now on.

And they will be. A woman is now Commander in Chief of the Army. A woman now takes precedence on every public occasion in Ireland where she is present. A section from the national anthem – "The Soldiers Song" – will be played whenever she arrives. It will be a woman who leads the nation in remembrance of the thousands of men who died for their country in the future. It will be a woman who represents Ireland at the enthronement of bishops and cardinals. It will be a woman who goes on to the field in Croke Park or Lansdowne Road to welcome and encourage the teams of young men who represent their country. In periods of celebration or mourning, on major national or international occasions, it will be a woman who speaks for us all.

Mary Robinson knows, and so do thousands of other women, that all of this cannot fail to make a difference. The presidency may be a symbolic office, but it also encompasses a range of other, equally potent symbols. And besides, in the phrase coined by Catherine Donnelly, an office is a place of work. In places of work all over Ireland, in homes, factories, and offices, there are women who feel differently today than they did at this time last year. Thousands of them have written to Mary Robinson since they elected her to tell her that – to tell her that her election was their personal statement about the future.

And about the past. On the first evening of the national tour, one of Mary's committee was standing in the crowd in Westport, savouring the atmosphere as hundreds of people clapped Mary to the echo. It was a remarkable sight. The strict instructions given by Michael Kilcoyne, who had organised the tour of Mayo (other than Ballina itself) were that the party must arrive in Westport to catch the crowd coming from the half-seven Mass on the Saturday evening. If Mary wasn't there by ten past eight at the latest, he had warned, the crowd would be gone, and the trip would be wasted.

But tours have a way of running late, and it was almost eight-thirty by the time the whole party arrived. Five hundred people had *waited* – in the open air, on a cold October evening – for Mary to arrive. It was unbelievable, perhaps the first big sign, a month before polling day, that there was more than frost in the air. There was magic too.

Four women stood in the centre of the crowd, dressed for the winter, one of them still with her missal under her arm. They listened attentively to everything Mary said, and clapped enthusiastically. Afterwards, they seemed to want to approach her, but, perhaps shy, hung back as she moved through the crowd. Mary spotted them, and came over and chatted for a few minutes. When she had moved on, the committee member who had been near them approached them to give them campaign leaflets.

"We don't need them," one of the women smiled at him, "sure we're voting for her anyway."

The committee member asked them if they would mind telling him why.

"Isn't she one of our own from Ballina," said one of the women. "And isn't she a woman," said another. The woman with the missal looked thoughtful for a moment, and then spoke.

"I voted Yes for the pro-life amendment," she said, "and No to divorce. And it's been on my conscience ever since. Voting for Mary now might undo some of the damage."

Before and after that incident, the support of women for Mary had become one of the most noticeable phenomena of the campaign. It showed up in the opinion polls – even those which showed Mary lagging behind Lenihan among male voters made it clear that she was scoring heavily among women voters. It showed up in the fund-raising – experienced participants could never remember a situation where so high a proportion of the money, perhaps a third in the end, had been sent in by women, often out of their housekeeping money and in not a few cases out of their pensions. It showed up in the attendances at public meetings, where women often outnumbered men by a margin of two to one.

But in the end, it has to be said, a quality of sympathy and compassion more marked among women than men almost undid Mary's chance of victory. There was a tangible feeling of sympathy among many women for the trauma that surrounded the last week of Brian Lenihan's campaign, and especially for the obvious suffering of his wife Ann. She had appeared on the Late Late Show with him in obvious pain and difficulty, almost breaking down under the pressure. She had been a lot more fluent and talkative on an earlier Late Late Show in May, when she had appeared in the early stages of the campaign to be interviewed about the book she had written on her husband's liver transplant operation. On the later show, her frayed emotions showed through clearly.

The last opinion poll of the campaign, prepared for the *Irish Times* on the two days after that Late Late Show, indicated that many women were wavering, torn between their commitment to Mary and the compassion that Ann Lenihan's loyalty and suffering undoubtedly inspired. Lenihan and Robinson were neck-and-neck amongst women voters in that poll, and had it not been for the famous attack on Mary by one of Lenihan's closest colleagues, Padraig Flynn, on the Saturday before polling, Lenihan might have been able to capitalise on that high level of compassion. As it was, Flynn's catastrophic blunder (dealt with in more detail later) restored the conviction many women already shared that a vote for Mary Robinson was vital, and drove indoors many thousands of other votes that might have made a difference to the Lenihan effort.

None of this stopped Fianna Fáil canvassers in particular from attacking Mary Robinson in the strongest possible way, and from trying to use the tactics of fear that had been so effective in the two referendum campaigns.

On the Monday night before polling, Fergus Finlay got a phone call from a journalist, who was outraged by a phone call she had herself just received from a close friend living in north county Dublin, who had within the previous five minutes been visited by two Fianna Fáil canvassers. These individuals had regaled the woman concerned with a whole series of absolutely untrue stories about Mary, and her secret plan to use the presidency to undermine the Constitution. These lies were compounded by the stories they told about Mary's personal life – also a tissue of lies.

Finlay was both astonished and angered. Finding it difficult to believe that Fianna Fáil would condone suggestions like this, he rang Fianna Fáil headquarters and asked to speak to Frank Wall, the General Secretary of that party. He explained what had happened, told him the exact location of the canvassers, and asked him to investigate. Wall's response was even more astonishing. He accused the Robinson campaign member of setting up the entire incident, and suggested that the call now being made was being taped!

On polling day itself, all parties testified to the number of women who were voting. There has never been an election in the state, in the view of most objective observers, in which the turnout of women was so high, in middle class and working class areas. And more than that – none of the parties outside the polling stations could ever remember an election in which so many women were declaring their intentions as they went in to vote.

At the end of that day, shortly before nine o'clock, the Mary Robinson canvassers outside the polling station at the technical school in Bray were preparing to tidy up and go home. Suddenly a young woman came running around the corner. She had a child in her arms, wrapped up against the cold, and another in the buggy she was pushing. "Is it closed?" she asked the canvassers, in a voice close to panic. "Is the polling closed?" No, they assured her, there was another five or six minutes to go. "Thank God!" she said. "The bastard. He never came home – and he promised me, tonight of all nights, he wouldn't be late ..."

Her husband had failed to come home in time to mind the kids, so that she could get out to vote. Frantic as the time got closer to nine, she had eventually bundled up the two children against the cold, and brought them with her. Among all the canvassers outside the station – Fianna Fáil, Fine Gael, Labour, and the Workers' Party – there was no doubt about who she was voting for.

"Not just partisans but patriots too"

Meathman Declan Geraghty is a founder member of the Progressive Democrats, and a member of their national council. He has been a friend and advisor to Mary Robinson for perhaps twenty years, and when he was asked to take charge of Mary's transport arrangements, and subsequently to co-ordinate her national tour, he agreed without hesitation. His commitment was to her rather than to any outmoded form of party politics, and to the whole notion of change that Mary's candidacy represented. Along with other senior PD people, he made strenuous efforts to persuade his party to support Mary publicly as many of them were prepared to do privately. But those efforts foundered on the PD's coalition commitments.

Throughout the tour, Declan represented the unflappable side of Mary's management team. The phrase "no problem" might have been invented for him, if it hadn't been appropriated by one of the opposition candidates! Whenever there was a row on the tour, it was almost always Declan who mediated, and he became adept at handling personnel problems. Those members of the team who had greeted him with dark suspicion, as a dreaded PD infiltrator, soon came to realise that his own politics had been left at the door of the bus, that his motivation was the same as everyone else's, and that his commitment was second to none. In fact, in common with a lot of other PD members, he had tried to persuade that party to come out publicly in support of Mary, although without success.

Barry Carey, on the other hand, had no politics. But when a driver was needed (for the first few months Nick had done all the driving until the risk of weariness had become too great), Barry had been asked to recommend someone, and had promptly volunteered himself. From the day he started on the campaign, the only time off that Barry took was to be with his wife for the birth of one of their children.

Nothing could upset him, or deter him from the task in hand. Generally he drove the Robinson's car, and when they were on the tour bus, would ensure that the car was always close at hand, in case Mary needed to make a quick dash to the next stop.

Barry had another area of expertise as well. He ran a company that specialised in highly sophisticated electronic equipment. Some of the people involved were worried about the possibility that the phone in Mary's home might be tapped, and Barry arranged to have it electronically swept. Although nothing was found, he took the precaution of installing "scrambler" devices in Mary's office at home, and in campaign headquarters and a number of other sensitive locations. He also carried one in the car, so that if they ever needed to ring home or campaign HQ from a hotel, it was a simple enough matter to ensure that the calls could not be listened to.

Declan and Barry, together with Aoife and Sinead (and Robert, the coach driver, on hire from Cronin's Coaches in Cork, who worked as hard as anyone and remained cheerful throughout the entire trip), were the core of the "road team". For long stretches, they were the only resources available to Mary – often the nearest thing she had to family on the road. The links that were forged between them will remain strong long after the memories of long days and very little sleep have faded.

In their own way, these four were typical of the kind of commitment that Mary was steadily attracting. Long before it was safe to regard her as a winner, she was surrounded by people willing to work incredible hours, living on chips and sandwiches, to get her elected. And these were not party people – indeed, for a lot of them, it was the first time that they had ever taken part in a campaign.

Men like John Gogan (or, as he was introduced to everyone, brother of Larry!), who arrived every morning in campaign headquarters at nine o'clock, and didn't leave very often until nine or ten at night. Women like Ita McAuliffe, who would do her own demanding full-time job all day, and then take home a huge pile of paperwork at night – bills, invoices, bank statements, cheque stubs – and work late into the night to ensure that the campaign was meeting all its financial obligations as it went along. People of all stripes and colours, committing time, expertise, initiative: Nora O'Neill, spending hours on the phone making "cold calls" to businessmen asking for money; Denise Brophy, devising and managing financial information systems; Suzie, making herself available for any job in headquarters, no matter how big or small.

Increasingly, the campaign attracted support from members of all parties and none. On the day before polling, a woman phoned Angie Mulroy in the campaign headquarters, and asked her to pass on a message to Mary. She introduced herself as a member of the De Valera family, and told her that many, if not most, of the family were going to vote for Mary. But long before that, the signs were there that Mary's campaign was breaking down the Civil War barriers.

It has been argued that one of the primary reasons for Austin Currie's failure in the campaign was the latent, and sometimes very overt, partitionist mentality among Irish people, who failed to see Currie as properly Irish simply because he came from north of the border. There is undoubtedly some truth in this – but the real truth is a lot more complex. Robinson campaign members can attest to meeting people who didn't regard Austin Currie as a proper Fine Gaeler, rather than a proper Irishman; and his lack of a political base in Ireland and within his own party was not something for which the Irish people deserved to be blamed. The truth of it was that more time was needed to sell the whole idea of Austin Currie – who had to spend the first half of his campaign doing nothing but introducing himself to his own party. If he had been nominated in April, at the same time as Mary was, he would have had some hope of making an impact – of putting down the roots that Mary had put down.

As it was, by the time a Fine Gael candidate was chosen, Mary had made considerable inroads into the Fine Gael vote. It would have taken a very special attraction – and probably someone who represented the same or a similar set of values as Mary did – to persuade Fine Gael voters to change their minds about supporting her. Even then, it will always be a matter of speculation if anyone could have won back half of the Fine Gael voters who opted for Mary. But the easy supposition that it was partitionism that did Currie in will always have to be questioned. After all, how could Mary Robinson have survived if old attitudes – the ones that dominated the divorce and abortion referenda, for instance, had surfaced?

In a way, the reasons for Fianna Fáil's failure in the campaign are easier to analyse. Long before the tapes scandal, their candidate was in trouble. From the very beginning, the Fianna Fáil campaign was totally complacent. At the start of the year, their calculation was that all Brian Lenihan had to do was to get himself nominated, and he would be a shoo-in for the Park. There was even expectation in some of the people around Lenihan at that time that he might emerge as an agreed candidate, and that he certainly wouldn't be seriously opposed.

In this calculation, of course, they weren't alone. When Mary Robinson's name emerged, newspaper editorials praised Dick Spring for ensuring that people would have a choice, but political commentators were unanimous as to who the choice would ultimately be. When Mary came into Leinster House for interviews on the day her name was floated, the media went through the motions. But they – and virtually everybody else – under-estimated the Irish people.

Mary Robinson was the first to discover that people really wanted a choice. Everywhere she went, she met people who were glad that she was there – that a candidate for high office had come to listen to them rather than to wave at them from a helicopter. The whole idea of a candidate listening rather than preaching, discussing rather than sloganising, was one of the two new elements she brought to Irish politics.

The other was her independence. She stood on a platform that everyone knew. Her background had been one that attracted the support of minorities, and as a result she had won many battles and lost many wars in the past. But she had never trimmed her sails, or changed or abandoned any of her values.

It has been said that there was a third element in Mary's campaign – the element of packaging. Fundamentally, it isn't true. Mary Robinson stood in front of her own platform. People could look at her and listen to her, and when they heard the vicious voices in their ears saying "This woman stands for abortion" or "This woman wants to break up families", they could see for themselves that it simply wasn't true. Since her election, Mary Robinson has been described by some as "a product". Some have argued that all that the losers have to do is to don the right suit of clothes, and they too will become winners. Others, eager to climb on the band-wagon of her success, have claimed that anyone could have won the presidency with the right handling touch. This is patent – and arrogant – nonsense, and all the more so when it comes from people who worked for Mary and recognised her intrinsic qualities and values.

Mary Robinson's attitude to the job she was applying for was this – if she was serious, she had to go for the interview as well-groomed as she would expect any other applicant to be. She knew that very often different standards are applied to women in seeking election – the candidate who is a man can turn up day after day in the same suit, and nobody will remark on it. But let the woman appear everywhere in the same clothes, and it will be assumed that she simply doesn't believe in taking good care of herself. This conditioning is something that Mary has fought against for years, and she is now in a better position to challenge stereotyped attitudes than she has ever been – precisely because she recognises the reality of them.

Because she is not an expert in the area – she has never worn make-up, and has been content with the sort of clothes that mark a woman out as a serious lawyer – she sought advice. The condition was this – under no circumstances was she prepared to wear clothes in which she was uncomfortable, and she was not prepared to be changed into something that she had never been. She consulted a lot of different people about clothes and make-up, deciding in the process that clothes have to be picked for a range of qualities – they had to be durable, capable of lasting a long day on a bus and not looking wrinkled at the end of it; they had to be comfortable; and they had to be Irish. She went to a top-class hairdresser, Alan Bruton, and listened carefully to what he had to say. What impressed her was his insistence that she should not try to change her features, just to show them off to better advantage. In the end, she agreed to a soft body wave, and was astonished – and pleased – with the result.

What emerged from the process was a stylish, elegant, attractive woman. But it was still Mary Robinson! All that had changed was that now more people could see how photogenic she had always been, because the hair that had previously hidden a fine-featured face was now swept away from it. In an era where people have their teeth capped and their noses turned up in order to look good, Mary Robinson had a hair-do. It has to be said that she was slightly uncomfortable with her new hair at first – but over time, the buzz of extra confidence that always comes with genuine compliments gave Mary an extra lift.

And undoubtedly the new look enabled people to listen to Mary without being distracted by thinking "Why doesn't she do something about her hair?" But hands up all those who voted for Mary Robinson because of her hair style and her clothes! Surely the truth of it is that people appreciated that she was prepared to make an effort to look her best when she came to see them, but that was as far as it went. If a hair-style can win the presidency, Des O'Malley might be in the Park instead of Mary.

The purpose of the changes that Mary made, and the kind of profile she adopted – and it is important to emphasise again that it was Mary who made the changes, and not any guru – was to ensure that when people came to judge her, they would be able to judge the whole of her. People who had known of Mary Robinson throughout her career didn't know she had three children, didn't know she was happily married to an attractive man, didn't know she was a Catholic, didn't know that her roots were in rural Ireland, didn't even know she could smile. They knew about the law, and they knew about Trinity – both rarefied and somewhat distant images, and neither of them telling the whole story. Mary didn't need anyone to tell her that if she was going to present herself to all the people of Ireland, the people would want to know about the real, the whole, Mary Robinson.

She herself had pointed out to those who approached her at the start that she could only stand as Mary Robinson, representing everything she had always represented – and frequently, that had not brought political popularity. The essential personal quality that she brought to the campaign was her integrity – and to suggest that she was in some way a cleverly-packaged product is to demean that integrity and the people who voted for it. It is also a considerable under-estimate of Mary's personal toughness for anyone to suggest that she could be persuaded to be something she isn't, or to adopt a pose for the sake of popularity. In fact, if Mary had been prepared to pose at any time in her twenty years of public life, she would surely have reached high office a long time before she did. Anyone looking at Mary Robinson's career can see that throughout her twenty years of public life, she espoused liberal values. She stood for change in attitudes to women and to equality, and on behalf of anyone discriminated against by or before the law. In that career, she built up a track record, on which she could be judged – and from which she could never escape, even if she wanted to.

But of course, she didn't want to. She brought the values she had always represented with her into the campaign, unflinching and unchangeable. She was ready to be judged on the basis of what she was and what she stood for, and nothing else. If the people didn't want what they saw, it was the right of the people to decide. And if nothing else – this time the people would have a choice.

For the first time in many years, it was a real choice, not just between parties and philosophies, but between real people and real attitudes. It wasn't an election about economics or about policy *per se* – and in a sense, that made the choice purer and starker.

Brian Lenihan was the prototype of a glad-handing politician, without an enemy in the world, and with a fund of well-meaning platitudes to offer for every situation. His phrase "No problem!" was legendary in politics, and his personal courage in facing terrible physical adversity added an extra dimension to the way in which he was viewed. The bonhomie for which he was famous had its down side – many viewers of the Late Late Show that had been devoted to him in early summer had been turned off by the stories told on the programme about how guards raiding a pub after hours had been offered "a pint or a transfer", and even more by the hilarity that such stories seemed to induce in the largely Fianna Fáil studio audience. From the start of the campaign, Lenihan had an unstated and unmeasured credibility problem – he had the reputation of always being the man that Fianna Fáil wheeled out whenever the indefensible had to be defended, and of being a party man first and foremost. Although universally liked, he had never inspired total respect.

Austin Currie, being a Northerner, brought an extra dimension to the choice available. Part of his difficulty was that neither he nor his party had a clear view on the extent to which that aspect of his persona should be emphasised. Initially, it seemed that there was an attempt to underplay his Northern origins, but that soon changed to an aggressive posture, perhaps based on Currie's own discovery, as he said frequently in the campaign, that he couldn't disown his origins – he only had to speak, and the accent would immediately mark him out. His appeal, other than within his own party, was somewhat nondescript – despite his years in Northern politics, he was not seen as a person who stood for something in terms of the issues of concern to the people of the Republic. This is a difficulty for all Northern politicians, simply because the politics of the North are seen as revolving around one issue only. In areas like health, education, employment, and so on, Currie had a major difficulty in convincing anyone that he had a track record – either of achievement or of protest – on which a judgement could be made about him.

Given the clarity of the choice, it would have been foolish in the extreme for anyone in the Robinson campaign to believe that the issues which surrounded Mary Robinson all her political life could be fudged, or that she could be presented in some way as other than she was. In fact, anyone from whom Mary asked advice offered the opinion that all of these issues should be confronted head on. Whether it was the case surrounding the students' right to information about abortion, or the Norris case involving the decriminalisation of homosexual activity, or campaigns on behalf of Travellers – all these issues were an integral part of what Mary stood for, and they couldn't, and wouldn't, be hidden away behind the body wave and the smart clothes. Eoghan Harris coined the phrase "the distortion issue" – a mix of divorce and abortion – and like Dick Spring before him and others later – advised Mary that she would have to deal with them early in the campaign. But no-one ever advised her to change, or to deny, her views – and she wouldn't have listened if they tried.

The assumption was made by some journalists early in the campaign – oddly enough, mainly by some women journalists – that Mary's stances on controversial issues in the past would be thrown out the window with the straight hair and the lawyers' suit. The same journalists were amazed later on when it became apparent that Mary was not prepared to trim her opinions on those issues, even at times when it looked as if they would get her into hot water. What they were missing was what Mary had picked up in her early travels around the country – that people on the ground were responding to her honesty and her forthrightness.

That's not to say that Mary had gone through her life unchanged and unchanging in all of her views. She had been at a stage in her life on the left of the Labour Party because of her frustration with what she saw as the compromises imposed by minority participation in Government. She had shared many political ideas with the left in general, particularly in the economic area. However, Dick Spring did not regard her as a socialist when he went to talk to her. There were many issues on which the two of them would not necessarily agree.

What was constant in Mary's life was her commitment to justice and to equality. The set of values that was bound up in that commitment was what attracted Dick Spring to her in the first place. And that was what she "sold" throughout the campaign – the values which were hers, and which people could respond to because they understood them and – even if they did not agree with them all – respected them.

People didn't support Mary Robinson because she was a socialist or a liberal or had good taste in hairdressers. They supported her because they understood her – understood her commitments to her own family, understood her need to speak plainly, understood the work she had been doing, understood the track record that she had built up over the years.

And they were refreshed by it, even, in many cases, exhilarated.

The choice they were being invited to make was made totally explicit by the directness and honesty of Mary's approach. The sense of style which the campaign brought out in her – and which never could have been brought out if it wasn't in her in the first place – supplemented the zest which her clarity and forthrightness generated. But it could never have been a substitute for it.

It was the real Mary Robinson that caught the public imagination – the lawyer and politician that they knew and respected, and the warm attractive woman that they liked. And it was the people of Ireland in the first place, and only them, who gave her the confidence to share herself totally with them.

Mary had been nominated by the Labour Party in April and by the start of October had been on the road for five months. There was also a formal nomination procedure to be gone through to comply with the requirements of the Constitution. She had to secure the names of at least twenty deputies and senators. When she went to the Custom House with her formal nomination papers they contained twenty-nine names showing a broad base of support – the seven Workers' Party deputies, senators David Norris and Brendan Ryan, and the twenty Labour parliamentarians.

But already by then she had secured the commitment of thousands of others, of all parties. Even if they couldn't legally sign her nomination form because they were private citizens and not TDs or senators, they were going to help her to make all the difference.

"A mandate for a changed approach"

The 4th of October was the day that the "mannerism yes" became an issue in the campaign. It was one of the two memorable phrases that will be remembered from the presidential election campaign, the other one being Brian Lenihan's "mature recollection". But it was the "mannerism yes" that for a few days gave nightmares to Mary Robinson and her team.

Campaign workers had been shaken out of their beds that morning by hearing Mary being reported as agreeing to open a condom stall in the Virgin mega-store, among other things. It wasn't on the news itself, but on It Says In The Papers, a review of the daily papers that appears after the 8 a.m. and 9 a.m. news bulletins. The newspapers in turn had apparently picked up the item from an interview Mary had given to *Hot Press* magazine, a weekly rock newspaper.

Sales of the magazine shot up that morning, as members of the campaign committee – several of whom had never seen the magazine before – rushed to buy it. One member rushed into 15 Merrion Square clutching his copy, which he had read on the DART. "Has anyone seen this?" he shouted. A chorus of voices answered "We're just reading it", as four other members held up the copies they had bought.

It was more dramatic even than it had appeared on the radio. Mary appeared in the article to be agreeing to open the condom stall as President – a completely illegal activity, since by law, condoms could only be sold in registered pharmacies, and the Irish Family Planning Association had already been prosecuted for running the stall in the Virgin Megastore. She had also said that as the elected President she would have the moral authority to look Charles Haughey as Taoiseach in the eye and tell him to "back off". She had described the Catholic church as being responsible for a good deal of the oppression of women. It seemed she had attacked the judiciary and the legal

114

profession, apparently agreeing with her interviewer that a lot of judges were ancient and sexist, and suggesting that male barristers in particular did a lot of their legal work – "exchanging briefs" she called it! – in the gents' toilet in the Four Courts. In short, the interview gave the impression that Mary had been swinging wildly all around her.

At least, at first glance it did. Nick and Mary, though, were adamant that she had been misrepresented in the interview, and that in particular she would never agree to commit illegal activity while as President – it went against everything she understood about the rule of law. The law was the law until legislators changed it, and those who make the law in a democracy can't break it.

So confident was Mary that she had been misrepresented – or at least misunderstood – that she agreed to go on the One O'Clock News to clear the matter up. She explained that she had a mannerism, when someone asked her a question, of prefacing her reply with the word Yes in order to indicate that she had understood the question, and she went on to say categorically that she would never do anything illegal as President.

Sometimes when you're in a hole, the best solution is to stop digging. Mary's attempts to clarify her position only muddied the situation more. *Hot Press* said they were standing over the interview in toto, and eventually made the tape of the interview available. Sections of it were broadcast on RTE and they showed that Mary had been quoted literally and correctly, although the discerning listener could easily detect that the Yes in question was indeed a mannerism rather than necessarily an affirmative answer. Nevertheless, the "mannerism yes" began to look like a very dangerous item, especially in a person who was noted for her clarity and care in dealing with language.

Some members of the committee believed that Mary had almost self-destructed, and that unlimited use would be made of the interview to raise all sorts of smears against her. There had been an expectation in the Robinson camp that the forces who had been involved in the divorce and abortion referenda would inevitably surface in a campaign against Mary, but no-one had quite expected that she would invite them in.

The national media were convinced that this was a major own goal. The *Irish Press* led the following day with the headline "Mary in Hot Water" in very large type, and most of the political correspondents freely wondered if it would be possible for her to recover from the damage. Everyone knew Mary's views on these issues, according to the logic of their argument, but what was the sense in her airing them so freely? Didn't everyone know that *Hot Press* spelled trouble, especially since Charles Haughey himself had been inveigled into saying in the magazine some years previously that he knew "some fuckers that he'd like to push over a cliff"?

It wasn't so much Mary's views that were being questioned, but her judgement in airing them so freely. It didn't matter that some of the people who were now criticising her were the same ones who had believed earlier that Mary would try to hide all her opinions once she became a candidate – the fact is that the media generally saw a candidate who had made a bad blunder. In their eyes she had offended against the conventional wisdom that there are certain targets that are too big for any politician to take on.

But a number of strange things started to happen. Spokespeople for the campaign were getting calls constantly, all of them from media people, suggesting that Robinson was suddenly in deep trouble. But there were no calls from the public, either to campaign headquarters or to Leinster House or to the Labour Party Head Office. In the three days or so that the controversy raged in the media – and it lasted from Thursday morning until the following Monday night – not one call came in from any member of the public complaining about the interview. The only calls – and they were from Robinson supporters – were arguing that Mary had been wrong to retract or clarify on the news.

In short, experts – both inside and outside the campaign – had got it wrong again. By the time that interview appeared – less than a month before polling day – Mary Robinson had already got her message across. Her work in establishing herself around the country, as someone who was direct and honest, now began to reap its own reward. When she appeared the following Monday night on the RTE Questions and Answers programme – the programme where Brian Lenihan was to shoot himself in the foot a fortnight later – it was noticeable that the audience listened with respect as she dealt with the issue. The attitude of the audience was well caught by Gerald Barry of the *Sunday Tribune*, another of the panellists, when he described the interview as an error of judgement, and then went on to say that Mary Robinson's record of work and achievement on behalf of oppressed people would be remembered long after the *Hot Press* gaffe had been forgotten.

There were elements of luck about that whole episode, it has to be said. The first opinion polls of the campaign proper were published on the Sunday and Monday after the *Hot Press* interview appeared; and they both showed that Mary was well ahead of Austin Currie and in second place, exactly the position that she needed to be in at that point. Both polls had been conducted prior to the *Hot Press* interview, and neither of them, naturally, gave any indication that the interview had damaged her in any way. But the good poll news added credibility in the eyes of the media to Mary's chances of winning, at just the moment when she needed that extra credibility, and drew the media's attention away from any lasting interest in *Hot Press*. Thus, the impression was subliminally created – entirely accidentally! – that the interview had done no damage to the candidate.

Secondly, the Fianna Fáil campaign was still at that point stultified by complacency. The media reported that Fianna Fáil strategists were rubbing their hands in glee at the self-inflicted damage of the *Hot Press* interview, but they never made the slightest effort to exploit it, because the strategy they were following consisted entirely of photo opportunities and bland speeches by Brian Lenihan – what the Americans call a "rose garden" strategy.

It was almost exactly a month later, on the Sunday before polling, that their first formal reaction to the interview came, when they wheeled out Colm Condon, a lawyer who had been Attorney General under Jack Lynch, to attack Mary over her *Hot Press* remarks about judges. The fact that he did it in front of a group called Lawyers For Lenihan, and that it was done only when Brian Lenihan was himself in the deepest trouble, made the attack extremely lame amd ineffective. The Taoiseach had several times in the intervening month, in the course of press conferences and briefings, made obvious, though oblique, references to the interview, when he said that the last thing the country needed was "an interfering President". But since references of that sort only conjured up images of his own (at the time!) very cosy relationship with Lenihan, it was counter-productive.

Fine Gael did try to exploit the interview, with Austin Currie putting out a statement that attacked Mary's remarks as divisive. But it was a mark of the trouble that the Fine Gael campaign was in that most media treated the Fine Gael attack as looking for attention, and it was far from prominently displayed.

The bottom line, though, has to be that the *Hot Press* interview, and the lack of public reaction to it, was a major sign that the times were changing. It is inconceivable to think that ten years, or even five years earlier, a person who was widely reported as expressing such forceful views could have emerged from the incident relatively un-scathed. The "mannerism yes" became a running joke on the campaign team – if someone promised that Yes, they would be in at eight o'clock the following morning, they were immediately asked if that was a "mannerism yes" or a real Yes.

But it was possible to laugh about it only because people generally accepted it for what it was. When they weighed up the views in the article against Mary's integrity and record, almost no-one came to the conclusion that she would be unfit for office on account of those views. She got a mandate from the people, holding and expressing her views, and that's why she was able to talk in the RDS about "a mandate for a changed approach".

Exactly the same thing applied to Brian Lenihan – only in reverse. When the "tapes" affair broke, his problem essentially was that he too had a track record. But unlike Mary Robinson, it was a track record of defending the indefensible, of saying "No problem" in any situation where there clearly was a problem. When he found himself in a situation where fudge and bluster wouldn't work, he had no other recourse.

The origins of the Lenihan tapes affair will be dealt with later, together with its impact on the Robinson campaign. It has been said of Brian Lenihan that he is the first politician in history to have been the victim of a smear campaign initiated by himself. He was odds-on favourite to win before the "tapes" affair, even though most Mary Robinson campaigners believe fervently to this day that Mary would have beaten him anyway, so great was the momentum that was building up behind the campaign. After the tapes affair, he was battling for his life, and he almost pulled it off only because of circumstances which generated a huge degree of sympathy for him as a victim and an underdog.

Again, the bottom line has to be that the times they are a'changing. One elderly woman was confidently approached by Fianna Fáil canvassers outside the polling station in Harold School in Dun Laoghaire on November 7th, and offered the Brian Lenihan literature. She angrily refused it, saying, "Indeed I will not take that! I've voted for Fianna Fáil all my life, but how could I vote for a man who looks out at me from the television and tells me whoppers! I'm voting for a woman who tells the truth, even if I don't agree with everything she says." And in she went, another vote for a changed approach.

Many members of the Workers' Party worked extremely hard for Mary, at national level and where the party was strong locally. In parts of the country, there was a certain amount of tension between Labour and WP people, but strenuous efforts were made by national figures in both organisations to convert these tensions into productive activity. In the Dublin area especially, the popularity of Workers' Party Deputies like Proinsias De Rossa, Pat Rabbitte, and Eamon Gilmore helped to establish a strong voting base under Mary. The work they did, and their commitment to her success, was entirely genuine.

But it had its down side too. It was Fine Gael, and specifically Austin Currie and Jim Mitchell, who introduced the "red scare" into the campaign. It was clearly done out of some desperation, and was incongruous in the extreme, coming from one man who had helped to found the Social Democratic and Labour Party in the North, and another who had been happy to work with the Labour Party for four years in Government. Indeed, one of the two men concerned admitted to a member of the Robinson team that attacking Mary Robinson because of her association with Labour, and more especially the Workers' Party, was a largely cynical exercise, made necessary because Fine Gael couldn't contemplate being beaten into third place. They couldn't beat her fair and square, so they had to drag her down, even if that alienated so many transfer votes that their man couldn't win anyway.

Despite the spurious nature of the attacks, there was fear in the Robinson camp that they might alienate some voters. At every opportunity, Currie emphasised such issues as De Rossa's affiliation to a communist group in the European Parliament, and they tried their best to paint Mary as a radical socialist who would use high office to nationalise banks and undermine the economy generally.

When Fianna Fáil took up this theme towards the end of the campaign, the belief grew in the Robinson camp that both bigger parties must be receiving intelligence through their private polling that the tactic was working.

In the course of exchanges in the Dáil about the incident in which the Taoiseach was alleged to have abused an army officer in Áras an Uachtaráin, Proinsias De Rossa made a remark to the effect that "After President Hillery retires and is succeeded by Mary Robinson, we'll be better able to investigate the entire incident". The Taoiseach seized on De Rossa's use of the word "we" to suggest that the Workers' Party had some kind of secret plot to take over control of the Áras. At Lenihan's final rally on the last Sunday before polling, the Taoiseach again attacked the left strongly, painting a picture of them as sinister and dangerous.

The next night, Fergus Finlay was alerted to the fact that all of the national newspapers would be carrying full-page advertisements the following day, the last day before polling. The advertisements would be based on the slogan "Is the left right for the Park?" and would include the message that "if you want to stop radical socialists taking over the Presidency", you should vote Fianna Fáil.

Finlay was alarmed, and consulted Bride Rosney and John Rogers. It had occurred to him that since the content of the ads was so obviously false and spurious, consideration could be given to some legal device for stopping them from appearing. The consensus of the other two was although it might be possible to prevent the ads from appearing, to take any action would probably ensure that the ads received more attention in the end than they would otherwise get, and could be seen as an over-reaction by the Robinson camp to a silly message.

They were right. The ads, when they appeared the following morning, were badly designed and badly laid out, guaranteed to have very little impact. The use of the "red-scare" tactic in the ads alone probably cost Fianna Fáil £40,000, and it was money down the drain.

But there was another lesson in it. It is not that long ago in Ireland when to be associated with the left was to be vulnerable to attack. The values that Mary Robinson espoused, from start to finish of the campaign, were not Fianna Fáil or Fine Gael values. Although she consistently refuses to allow herself to be labelled, there is no doubt in Ireland about where she stands in any debate between rich and poor, between haves and have-nots, between privileged and under-privileged, between charity and rights – and yes, between left and right.

She has been elected as the first citizen of Ireland by people who know her views, who respect the integrity with which she holds those views, and who will always know where she stands, no matter how constrained she might be in the future. They elected a person who is radical, committed to change, and determined to bring a different approach to her office. It is an approach which will enable the office to stand as a symbol of change, and will enable her to confront hide-bound attitudes without confronting constitutional imperatives.

The people gave her a mandate for that changed approach, and all the signs are that the people will be with her all the way.

"Nothing rational or reasonable"

Thursday, October 25th, was the day that the Fianna Fáil onslaught began. It continued mercilessly until the Saturday before polling day, a total of ten days. All of the might that the Robinson campaign had been fearing for months was suddenly unleashed. But to everyone's amazement, it was unleashed by Fianna Fáil against itself. They rolled out all their biggest guns, and pointed them straight at their own feet.

The Robinson team had been waiting for months, especially since the publication of the *Hot Press* interview, for a Fianna Fáil offensive. So many issues had been raised in that interview alone, so many hostages to fortune given, so many potential constituencies offended, that it was inexplicable to the Robinson campaign that Fianna Fáil largely chose to ignore it. The only possible explanation lay in the assumption that the Lenihan camp was complacent to the point of arrogance – and it was that complacency that was to prove their undoing.

It had started innocently enough, on the Questions and Answers programme of Monday 22nd. The panel had been expected to consist of Brian Lenihan, Jim Mitchell, Michael D Higgins, and Nuala O'Faolain. At the last moment, Jim Mitchell was withdrawn and Garret FitzGerald put in in his place. The only clue to Fine Gael's intentions in making this switch lay in a statement issued by FitzGerald in the afternoon, which accused Lenihan of "persistently" making improper phone calls to President Hillery in 1982, to try to prevent the dissolution of the Dáil at the time. Because of the suddenness with which the switch was made, there had been no time to forewarn Michael D Higgins, who was representing the Robinson campaign on the panel. He had earlier been advised that the campaign did not want Brian Lenihan unduly harassed on the programme – the committee's calculation was that the studio audience was likely to be hostile to him anyway, and nothing should be done which would generate sympathy for him.

In the event, Lenihan seemed to acquit himself reasonably well, apart from a complete misunderstanding of the powers of the presidency in relation to a dissolution of the Dáil. FitzGerald gave what seemed like a typical performance, with a lot of huffing and puffing about the events of eight years earlier. Lenihan had denied making any phone calls to the President in 1982.

As events were to show, it was Brian Lenihan who had scored the direct hit – on himself. In the course of the following day, Fergus Finlay was told that there was a tape in existence, which would prove that Lenihan had told lies on the programme about his part in the events of 1982. It was immediately assumed that the tape must be in the possession of Fine Gael, and the committee tried to prepare itself for a shock revelation by Fine Gael in the Dáil. It was a worrying moment – the high drama of Dáil chamber revelations was just the shot in the arm that the Fine Gael campaign needed. The scenarios painted included the image of the Fine Gael leader Alan Dukes bringing a tape recorder into the Dáil, and forcing yet more denials from the Fianna Fáil front bench before playing the tape.

Intensive enquiries during the day satisfied the committee that Fine Gael had no tape – in fact, before the day was out, it was clear that Fine Gael were frantically looking for it. Strong denials by the Taoiseach and by the Government Press Secretary that any phone calls had been made in 1982 seemed to kill the story – except that it now emerged that the *Irish Times* was very confident that it had unimpeachable sources for continuing to assert that the calls had been made.

On Thursday, the bomb exploded in Fianna Fáil's face. At a press conference organised by the *Irish Times*, the student who had made the tape, Jim Duffy, played a recording of Brian Lenihan apparently boasting that not only had he tried to ring the President, but had actually spoken to him.

Without any time to prepare a response, the Fianna Fáil campaign team rushed Lenihan to the RTE studios to appear on the Six-One

News. The Robinson campaign team watched in astonishment as Lenihan solemnly turned away from Sean Duignan, the interviewer, and faced the cameras to intone that on mature recollection he was now assuring the Irish people that in effect he had not told the truth to Jim Duffy six months previously.

There were divided views in the Robinson committee. Some wanted to go on the offensive immediately, in the belief that this development would breathe new life into the Fine Gael campaign. Mary Robinson herself, who had spent the day campaigning in Dublin, and had no time to think, acted instinctively, and effectively pre-empted the discussion raging among members of the committee. She quite simply felt a lot of human sympathy for the dilemma in which Lenihan had placed himself, and that's what she expressed.

Clearly, the issue of Lenihan's credibility was now at the top of the agenda, and likely to remain so for the remainder of the campaign. But she felt strongly that that was a matter on which the view of the people would emerge quickly, and that it was not an appropriate moment to be seeking to make capital.

Other members of her campaign team were not so sure. As the weekend loomed up, the fear among some members of the committee was that the campaign could become marginalised, and that the issue at stake was one where the traditional rivalry between Fianna Fáil and Fine Gael in the Dáil could reassert itself, leading to a situation where Currie could start to eat into the opinion poll lead that Mary Robinson enjoyed over him.

There was an element of panic in this response, partly caused by the fact that many members of the committee were closeted in offices and meeting rooms all day long, unable to take an accurate pulse of public reaction. Not for the first time, team members wished for the resources to be able to undertake instant market research, so that they could make some kind of scientific judgement about how the developing situation was affecting the campaign.

The absence of adequate information led to a strategic mistake. A member of the committee, who was also on Dick Spring's staff, was told by an RTE reporter that both Fine Gael and the Workers' Party had put down motions of no confidence in the Government on the Friday evening. Fearing marginalisation, he instantly replied that Labour would be putting down a motion also.

Spring had made no such decision. His reasoning, which he had discussed with other deputies, was that the events of the two days, and the obviously incredible position that Lenihan was in, would leave the Fianna Fáil candidate increasingly isolated as time went on. Already, the look of despair on campaign manager Bertie Ahern's face every time he appeared in public was revealing signs of considerable strain in the Fianna Fáil camp – a strain that was accentuated when Lenihan first announced that he was going to ask the President to confirm that no phone calls had been made, and then, under obvious pressure from Ahern, withdrew that intention the following day. If this kept up, the Lenihan campaign would begin to unravel very quickly.

A No Confidence debate, on the other hand, would force Fianna Fáil to rally around him, and would place the junior partner in Government, the Progressive Democrats – many of whom were closet Robinson supporters – in an impossible position. They would have to vote for the Government, and thereby lend credence to Lenihan's position. In the absence of any such debate, the damage to Lenihan's credibility would become the paramount issue of the remainder of the campaign.

In the event, it didn't really matter. Once a motion of confidence had been put down – no matter what the source – Labour, in common with all of the other opposition parties, had no choice but to vote against the Government. Nevertheless, Spring's reasoning – and the private rebuke he delivered to his staff member – was to prove soundly based. Even though it was impossible to predict the actual outcome of the confidence debate, it *did* almost save Lenihan's campaign in the end.

By the time the debate started in the Dáil, confidence in the Robinson camp had got another boost. Most members of the committee had gone to Limerick and Kerry that weekend as Mary's national tour left Dublin again, and the feeling on the streets was palpable. All over the South West, people came out to see Mary, to shake her hand, and to hear her speak.

There was a slightly unpleasant incident in Listowel, when Mary posed for photographers on the bar of a bicycle to which someone had strapped a toy telephone. Some members of her committee were horrified when Mary playfully lifted the phone and pretended to make a call. They were convinced that the resulting photographs would be used to portray Mary mocking Brian Lenihan's difficulties. A row ensued, with Mary taking a dim view of the over-protectiveness of the people around her.

Good humour was restored when, in Tralee town, in teeming rain late on the Saturday afternoon, nearly 2,000 people congregated to hear Mary speak from the back of a lorry in the middle of the main street. She refrained from mentioning the tapes affair, as she had all weekend, and concentrated instead on the by now well-tried speeches outlining the positive aspects of her own campaign. The reception was tumultuous, as it had been right through the weekend. There was very little doubt that whoever had been damaged by the controversy, it was not Mary Robinson. And the offending photographs taken earlier never appeared in any of the national newspapers!

If scientific proof of the growing momentum of the campaign were needed, it came on Sunday, with the publication of a poll conducted by Irish Marketing Surveys that showed that no more than 18 per cent of the people believed Brian Lenihan's current version of the "phone calls to the President affair". More importantly, 51 per cent of the people polled were now expressing the intention to vote for Mary on November 7th. This was an unbelievable figure, almost reversing the most recent poll (taken before the phone calls affair broke) which had given Lenihan a comfortable lead. But the figures in the poll did little more than bear out the atmosphere that Mary and her team had detected on the streets over the previous few days.

It was Mary herself who warned the campaign committee that what the polls were now showing represented considerable volatility among the electorate. "If he can go down so quickly, it's entirely possible that he could come up again," she said again and again, always cautioning against any assumption that the campaign was now over. For her own part, she agreed to a number of previously unscheduled interviews and media appearances, and began looking for more opportunities to meet people. Since she was already very tired, this was almost to prove a serious mistake.

Meanwhile, the confidence debate in the Dáil was providing high drama. It had emerged that the Progressive Democrats were not automatically going to vote with Fianna Fáil, arguing that Lenihan's actions had damaged the credibility of the Government. It was widely assumed that they had demanded Lenihan's resignation, although in fact they had tabled no specific demand. One of the campaign team was told that they had privately and informally given the Taoiseach a number of options, including the holding of a public enquiry into the whole affair.

Whatever was demanded, it was Lenihan's head that was delivered. On Wednesday morning the Taoiseach had defended him emphatically in the Dáil debate, but by that night he had fired him, after Lenihan had refused to resign. In that debate, the Taoiseach had also denied emphatically a further charge that had emerged – that he personally had abused an army officer in Áras an Uachtaráin on the night in question in 1982, and had threatened his career if the officer refused to put his phone calls through to the President.

Several members of the campaign committee had received phone calls about this allegation, all from former army officers, and all asserting that the allegation was true, but none was able to produce any documentation. Subsequent attempts to question the Taoiseach and other relevant ministers about the matter in the Dáil were all ruled out of order.

The net effect of the entire episode was that the man who had been Tánaiste when the campaign started was now a back-bench Fianna Fáil deputy, although still the party's candidate for the Presidency. It was clear now that the contest was a two-horse race, and that one of the horses had been badly wounded coming down the home straight. But it was equally clear that the Fianna Fáil organisation was at last beginning to wake up. Everywhere Lenihan went, he was surrounded by huge throngs of party well-wishers, and the media was speculating hourly that sympathy for him and for his family could overcome his enormous credibility problem.

Mary had been scheduled to do a major interview for Today Tonight on the previous Thursday, the day that the tape was played to an incredulous public (Lenihan and Currie had done similar interviews earlier). Because of the controversy that had ensued, Today Tonight had asked that the interview be postponed. Although Mary was entitled, under RTE's obligation to provide balanced coverage, to insist that the interview go ahead, she agreed to its postponement until the following Tuesday. It was to be recorded in Waterford late on Tuesday afternoon and transmitted that night.

That meant that in the last full week of the campaign, Mary would have three extensive media opportunities – the Today Tonight interview on Tuesday, the debate between the three candidates on Thursday (also on Today Tonight), and the Late Late Show on Friday – while the other two candidates only had the latter two opportunities to make ground. What's more, she was going into that last full week as the clear front runner. It should have been a ready-made formula for success – in fact, the strain was almost too much, and the burden of being a front-runner led to Mary making her first major mistakes since the *Hot Press* interview in early October.

The first interview, though, was an extraordinary success. A very full schedule had been arranged for the Tuesday, taking in campaign stops in north Cork, the whole of South Tipperary, and Waterford city and county. To make room for the interview, the schedule was compressed, though not altered. By the time Mary faced Brian Farrell and his camera crew, she had already put in a gruelling day, and still had to address a major public meeting in the city that night.

It was by no means the best way to prepare for an interview, and Mary knew in advance that Brian Farrell was going to ask her searching questions about some of the subjects that had been raised in the *Hot Press* interview, and about her legal work, including her participation in the students' "Right to Information" legal actions.

Once again, Fianna Fáil came to the rescue. Anne Byrne, a member of the campaign team who was travelling on the bus that day, had told Mary about remarks made by John Browne, a Fianna Fáil deputy from Wexford, at a campaign meeting in the Talbot Hotel in Wexford at which Brian Lenihan had been present.

"She's the biggest hypocrite in the campaign," Browne was reported in the *Wexford People* as shouting to the hysterical crowd. "She's pro-divorce, pro-contraception, and pro-abortion. Is she going to have an abortion referral clinic in Áras an Uachtaráin? That's what I'd like to know."

Those who were on the bus, including some who had been there for the entire trip, had never seen Mary so annoyed. One of the team remarked afterwards that John Browne's body would have adorned the campaign bus if he had been within reach. She issued an immediate statement demanding a retraction and apology – but although Browne was to admit to his local paper the day after polling that he had "gone over the top", the apology was never forthcoming.

The anger she felt at one of the most filthy smears of the entire campaign sustained her through the Brian Farrell interview. Her anger, controlled and yet tangible, came across in the interview, and enabled her to deal with the whole issue of abortion and the right to information forcefully and with absolute clarity. When it was broadcast, members of the committee who had watched believed it to have been the best interview given by any candidate for office for many years. There was no fudge, no dodging difficult issues, just Mary setting out her position honestly, directly, and with passion.

But after it was over, Mary was in a state of considerable exhaustion. The anger that had sustained her through a difficult day and a tough interview was replaced by a physical and mental fatigue. She had been on the road for six months, in every part of the country, and had met thousands of people. She had done twenty five miles of a marathon run, but now she had hit the wall that marathon runners fear so much. The other two candidates, much later into the race, were obviously fresher, and she imagined them beginning to breathe down her neck. She began to think that the end would never come.

She went through the following day in a daze. It was Wednesday, the day of the Dáil confidence debate, and she spent much of the time – in common it seemed with the entire population of Wexford county – trying to keep abreast of the unfolding drama in Dublin. For a good deal of the day, it seemed that the Government would fall on the motion, and nobody could tell her with any confidence that a general election would not affect the outcome of the presidential election. In her own opinion a general election would be disastrous, and would ensure that nobody bothered to vote at all on November 7th.

The actual outcome was almost as bad from Mary's point of view. Instead of the Government collapsing, the debate ended with the Taoiseach announcing that he had dismissed Brian Lenihan from the Cabinet, and the former Tánaiste was immediately photographed being carried shoulder-high across the front of Leinster House to an office across the road, where he gave a fighting press conference announcing that he would carry on to victory. The sight of the sacked Brian Lenihan, surrounded by hundreds of well-wishers and looking younger, fitter, and more determined than she felt, made her begin to regret her decision to stand aloof from the controversy that had surrounded him for the previous week. She began to calculate that by showing her own instinctive human sympathy, she had encouraged others to feel sympathetic too. Now she felt that if the Government and Fianna Fáil could dispense with him, that made him "fair game" for attack.

As the bus made its way back to Dublin on Thursday, stopping in all the major towns on the way, Mary wrestled with a decision. She now believed that in the debate that night on RTE, she would have to take Brian Lenihan on. She no longer felt like a front-runner, but that she was beginning to falter, and that Lenihan in particular was catching up fast. Physically and mentally, she was exhausted. She had come so far, so close to doing the impossible, and she could feel it slipping away.

Already, she was investing all her hopes in one more good performance, and in the possibility that she could destroy Lenihan's credibility once and for all. She was a top-class lawyer, after all, and if anyone could put Lenihan through the hoops, she could.

There is a conventional wisdom in politics that when you are the front runner, you follow the "three Ks" – keep moving, keep smiling, keep quiet. To do it effectively, the candidate in the lead must know that he or she is in the lead. The corollary, of course, is that "when you've got nothing, you've got nothing to lose".

When her campaign team gathered in Mary's house that night, to discuss the debate with her in advance, nobody counselled Mary against abandoning her front-running position. And nobody warned her that there would be a participant in the debate with "nothing to lose" – Austin Currie. The basic assumption that had been made about Currie was that he no longer mattered, and that in any event he would be more interested in damaging Lenihan than in attacking Robinson. He had after all been stressing the common ground that lay between himself and Robinson for the previous few weeks.

The balance of advice that she received instead before the programme was that if she wanted to attack Lenihan, there was a right way and a wrong way to do it. If he came on the programme looking and sounding like a wounded animal, it would be counterproductive for her to go after him. If on the other hand she could establish, to her own satisfaction and that of the audience, that he was vigorous and fit, there would then be an opportunity for her to say that she was glad that he had not suffered unduly from the traumatic effects of the previous few days, and that there was now no need to pull her punches. If she could get that message across *first*, she need then feel no inhibitions about attacking him.

Shortly before the group left to go to the television studios, the phone rang. It was Eoghan Harris. She took the call, and in his usual rapid-fire fashion he told her that the time had come to go for Lenihan bald-headed. Take the gloves off, he told her, and don't pussyfoot around – otherwise you'll let him re-establish some credibility. As an experienced professional, Harris would know that the last piece of advice she received before the programme would stick in Mary's mind. Coming so close to the programme, and allowing her no time to weigh up his advice, it was the worst thing Harris could have done.

It had been decided before the programme, apparently by drawing lots, that Olivia O'Leary would address the first question to Mary. Mary didn't know that in advance, but had already made up her mind that whatever she was asked, she would turn it into an attack on Lenihan. To the amazement of most people watching, that is precisely what she did, and the hour-long debate was six minutes under way before Austin Currie got a look in, so busy were Mary and Lenihan discussing the former Tánaiste's credibility.

But Mary had overdone it. Her attack sounded sharp to most people, and contrasted very badly with the dignified stance that she had adopted up to then. She had also miscalculated – as had the people advising her beforehand – forgetting that the presence of a third candidate entitled to equal time would rob her of the opportunity to put Lenihan under cross-examination. In effect, she had prepared for a debate between the two of them, figuring that Currie didn't matter.

But when Currie did get involved, it was Mary to whom he devoted most of his attack, accusing her of being in thrall to communists and others. Although it was clearly a farcical charge – especially coming from a founder member of the SDLP – Mary was rattled by it. And when Olivia O'Leary chose to pursue the issue of Mary's commitment to socialist values, Mary decided under pressure to reject the socialist label, as she had consistently rejected labelling throughout the campaign. Had she been thinking on her feet, as she admitted later privately, she would have tried to define a set of values rather than reject a set of values. The candidate who had been so impressive at explaining the values she represented on television two nights before now looked distinctly uncomfortable when very similar questions were put to her.

Mary was tense after the programme, but not distraught. One member of the committee who made a number of quick phone calls to establish some kind of feedback got a very mixed reception from the people he rang, although nobody said it was disastrous. Lenihan was pleased with himself in the hospitality room after the programme, knowing that he had come through it looking fit and sounding strong. The Currie camp was convinced that their man had done best of all, and that the result was bound to increase his vote share.

By the following day, Mary felt she was in deep trouble. Although the media reaction was mixed – with the majority of the newspapers declaring Currie the winner – the general feeling was that she had blown it by so nakedly attacking Lenihan, and had managed to attract even more sympathy for him. Just as bad, members of the left-wing parties who had supported her were outraged at her apparent efforts to put as much distance as possible between them and her. Phone calls were coming in from people who had been working at night on her behalf, and who would be badly needed on polling day, to say how upset they were at her total refusal to recognise the socialist label. Even those who understood why it was necessary for her to reject labels – who had accepted her in the knowledge that she wasn't a socialist – felt that she had handled the situation with a complete lack of tact or grace.

The upshot was that Mary went into the Late Late Show that night more convinced than ever that she had ground to make up, and with a lot of feedback telling her that she had to make amends to her left-wing supporters.

Nick Robinson was particularly worried about the Late Late Show, on which he too had to appear, together with the other candidates' spouses. He had very little television experience – certainly none where the stakes were so high – and felt at a disadvantage competing against two wives. He was also afraid of coming across as very "Dublin 4", middle class and out of touch. He knew that Mary was under enough pressure without a bad performance by him on the programme.

He asked Eoghan Harris to help him to prepare. Harris worked with him for several hours that day, talking to him about body language, the importance of humour, the need to modulate the voice differently for television.

In the course of the session, Nick told a story about how as a young solicitor he had been asked to help the dying Seamus Ennis, the famous piper, to make a will. Ennis wanted it written into his will that he was bequeathing his pipes to Liam Óg Ó Floinn, "because he knew how to play them". Harris encouraged Nick strongly to tell the story on the programme, and they discussed ways of ending it, so that Nick could point to the story as a good reason for voting for Mary.

In the end, Nick, using his own judgement, told the story to considerable effect on air, and ended by saying that that was how he believed *each* of the candidates should be judged – the one best able to play the pipes should be the one to get them. His performance was judged by many to have been outstanding.

But in some ways, his was much the easier role to play. Although Mary did better than she had done the previous night (and duly made amends to her left-wing supporters by mentioning Dick Spring and the left-wing parties several times) there was very little of the vitality and warmth that had characterised the rest of the campaign. Once again, Currie's team was jubilant, believing that he and his wife Anita had made the best use of the programme, and convinced that even at this late stage, two good television appearances were bound to do him good.

Fine Gael had another strategy as well. They knew that apart from the many Fine Gael voters who had switched to Mary out of admiration for her and what she stood for, a great many of their supporters had abandoned Currie as a lost cause, and were voting for Robinson as the best way of beating Lenihan. They calculated that a formal vote transfer arrangement between Robinson and Currie would enable many traditional votes to come back to Fine Gael, on the basis that they could vote One for Currie and then transfer their second preferences to Robinson.

The Robinson camp had resisted such an arrangement for several weeks, largely out of fear of diluting Mary's strong individual appeal. Now, late on the Friday night, the reasoning was that there was very little to lose by such an arrangement. If Lenihan was closing the gap, as feared, the election would ultimately depend on getting the absolute maximum number of second preference votes from Currie. The committee believed that even if Currie did cut Mary's lead, it was too late for him to eliminate it.

Accordingly, a statement was jointly drafted at around one in the morning between members of Currie's campaign team, who were operating from a suite in the Berkeley Court Hotel, and a member of the Robinson team operating from his home. When the statement was completed the following morning it emerged that although it had to be cleared with Mary Robinson, and that Dick Spring would also be consulted, on the Robinson side, there was surprisingly no necessity for the statement to be seen by Alan Dukes.

A photocall was arranged for the Saturday afternoon in Stephen's Green, but by the time it took place, Fianna Fáil had once again shot itself in the foot, this time with devastating accuracy. The perpetrator was Padraig Flynn, Minister for the Environment, who had gone on radio to damage Mary Robinson, and probably ended up sealing the election for her.

The panel discussion Rodney Rice's Saturday View programme involved Flynn, speaking from RTE's Castlebar studios, together with Brendan Howlin, the Labour TD for Wexford, and Michael McDowell, the Chairman of the Progressive Democrats, both of whom were listening to him in the Montrose studios.

About half-way through the programme, Flynn suddenly launched into a vitriolic attack on Mary.

"She was pretty well constructed in this campaign by her handlers the Labour Party and the Workers Party," he said. "Of course it doesn't always suit if you get labelled a socialist, because that's a very narrow focus in this country – so she has to try and have it both ways. She has to have new clothes and her new look and her new hairdo and she has the new interest in family, being a mother and all that kind of thing. But none of us you know, none of us who knew Mary Robinson very well in previous incarnations ever heard her claiming to be a great wife and mother."

At this point McDowell tried to interrupt, but nothing could stop the Minister.

"Mary Robinson reconstructs herself to fit the fashion of the time" (Brendan Howlin – "That's outrageous"), "so we have this thing about you can be substituted at will, whether it's the pro-socialist thing, or pro-contraception, or pro-abortion – whatever it is." (Howlin again – "That's outrageous and desperate.") "But at least we should know. Mary Robinson is a socialist, she says it and has admitted it previously. Now she may have changed her mind, and if she has changed her mind so be it. But at least she should tell us that she has changed her mind, and not be misleading us."

According to one person watching from the control room, McDowell's face was a study as he listened to the attack. When Flynn had finished, and before Howlin could respond, McDowell exploded. He demanded that the Minister have some manners for once, and called his attack on Mary "disgusting".

The effect was sensational. Mary was canvassing in Grafton Street at the time, and hadn't heard the programme. But she was approached in the street by two people she vaguely recognised. They introduced themselves to her as people she had met in RTE on a previous occasion when she had sat on a panel with Seamus Brennan, the Fianna Fáil minister. They had been there in the audience as close friends and supporters of Brennan – but now, after what Padraig Flynn had just said on the radio, they had decided that they were determined to vote for her.

Between finishing her canvass in the Grafton Street area and the photocall with Currie, there was time for a quick lunch in the Unicorn Restaurant just off Merrion Row. By the time she got there, she had been fully briefed on the programme, which was just as well, since the first person she met in the restaurant was McDowell, who had just arrived in from RTE. Someone had handed Mary a doll in the course of the walkabout, and smiling broadly, she presented him with it, saying, "I heard you were left holding the baby!" When she got back to her own table, she remarked to the other people present, "With enemies like Michael, who needs friends!"

By the time of the photocall, word had come through that Flynn had phoned in an effusive apology, which would be carried on all news bulletins for the next twenty-four hours. Word too had reached the campaign of a new opinion poll, due to be published the following day, which showed Mary still slightly ahead of Lenihan, and Currie still languishing in a poor third place – his good television showing had come too late to save him.

It was a happy Mary Robinson who shared the cameras with Austin Currie that Saturday afternoon. It had been the longest ten days of her life. In the sporting cliché, she had almost peaked too soon. Physically worn out, and mentally exhausted, the photographers were still able to capture a brighter smile than had been there for a week. The campaign which most of its participants thought was in trouble was back on track for the final run in. And it was thanks to a considerable extent to "the might, money, and merciless onslaught" of Fianna Fáil!

"Look what you did"

On the second day of the count, in the RDS in Dublin, exactly 41,732 votes went missing. At least, the figures posted up on the notice boards around the RDS were smaller by that amount than the figures reported overnight in the newspapers. And even worse – Mary's lead over Brian Lenihan had been cut by nearly 3,000 votes!

It was one of the tallymen, Frank Butler, who spotted what had happened. The number of "missing" votes corresponded exactly with the total vote reported from the Wicklow Constituency. When Ruairi Quinn pointed out the discrepancy and its source to the national returning officer, Tim Sexton, the error was quickly rectified, and the correct official figures were there for all to see.

Two out of every three Irish people cast their votes on November 7th. Of the total, 612,265 cast them for Mary Robinson. She was 82,219 votes behind Lenihan on the first count, but Austin Currie's 267,902 votes were still to be distributed – and tallymen all around the country had reported that they were going so heavily in Mary's favour that victory was assured.

The final opinion poll of the election had shown Mary and Lenihan neck-and-neck at 43 per cent, with Currie at 14 per cent. Although Lenihan had come in on the day with his vote slightly over the predicted figure, Mary had slipped back a little, losing four points while Currie had gained three to finish with 17 per cent. The most likely explanation was that the "transfer pact" agreed between them and heavily publicised over the last weekend, had encouraged some Fine Gael voters, previously committed to Mary, to "go home", voting One for Currie and Two for Robinson. The pact had almost certainly deprived Mary of any chance she might have had of a first-round lead – but it had ensured that Fine Gael voters were to transfer to her by a margin of more than five to one across the whole country.

Nationally, after all the votes were counted and second preferences distributed, Mary had won by a margin of **86,557** – that was the difference between her 817,830 votes, and Lenihan's 731,273. The margin of victory was eight times bigger that Eamon DeValera had secured in 1966! On a constituency by constituency basis, this is how the people voted:

Carlow/Kilkenny: (Total poll 66.5%)	First Count	Second Count
Currie	9941 (18.8%)	
Lenihan	23808 (45.1%)	+ 1295 = 25103 (48.4%)
Robinson	19054 (36.1%)	+ 7679 = 26733 (51.6%)
Robinson wins		

Cavan/Monaghan (Total poll 62.1%)	First Count	Second Count
Currie	10049 (21.2%)	
Lenihan	25365 (53.6%)	+ 1431 = 26796 (57.7%)
Robinson	11923 (25.2%)	+ 7741 = 19664 (42.3%)
Lenihan wins		

Clare (Total poll 67.3%)	First Count	Second Count
Currie	7956 (18.3%)	
Lenihan	21669 (50.0%)	+ 1046 = 22715 (53.2%)
Robinson	13745 (31.7%)	+ 6259 = 20004 (46.8%)
Lenihan wins		

Cork East (Total poll 67.6%)	First Count	Second Count
Currie	7048 (18.5%)	
Lenihan	16928 (44.4%)	+ 908 = 17836 (47.9%)
Robinson	14124 (37.1%)	+ 5314 = 19438 (52.1%)
Robinson wins		

Cork N.C. (Total poll 62.0%)	First Count	Second Count
Currie	6038 (15.5%)	
Lenihan	15020 (38.6%)	+ 914 = 15934 (41.6%)
Robinson	17832 (45.9%)	+ 4514 = 22346 (58.4%)
Robinson wins		

Cork N.W. (Total poll 74.3%)	First Count	Second Count

Currie	8414 (27.7%)		
Lenihan	13843 (45.5%)	+ 1053 =	14896 (50.3%)
Robinson	8162 (26.8%)	+ 6549 =	14711 (49.7%)

Lenihan wins

Cork S.C.	First Count	Second Count	
(Total poll 68.0%)			
Currie	9254 (17.2%)		
Lenihan	18176 (33.9%)	+ 1240 =	19416 (36.8%)
Robinson	26226 (48.9%)	+ 7075 =	33301 (63.2%)

Robinson wins

Cork S.W.	First Count	Second Count	
(Total poll 69.3%)			
Currie	8623 (29.1%)		
Lenihan	11957 (40.4%)	+ 1127 =	13084 (45.6%)
Robinson	9034 (30.5%)	+ 6606 =	15640 (54.4%)

Robinson wins

Donegal N.E.	First Count	Second Count	
(Total poll 51.2%)			
Currie	3958 (17.1%)		
Lenihan	12834 (55.3%)	+ 550 =	13384 (59.4%)
Robinson	6397 (27.6%)	+ 2765 =	9162 (40.6%)

Lenihan wins

Donegal S.W.	First Count	Second Count	
(Total poll 53.3%)			
Currie	4794 (19.0%)		
Lenihan	13344 (53.0%)	+ 572 =	13915 (56.5%)
Robinson	7058 (28.0%)	+ 3672 =	10730 (43.5%)

Lenihan wins

Dublin Central	First Count	Second Count	
(Total poll 59.6%)			
Currie	4711 (12.3%)		
Lenihan	17855 (46.7%)	+ 793 =	18648 (49.5%)
Robinson	15683 (41.0%)	+ 3359 =	19042 (50.5%)

Robinson wins

Dublin North	First Count	Second Count	
(Total poll 66.0%)			
Currie	3931 (11.4%)		
Lenihan	14812 (43.1%)	+ 646 =	15458 (45.4%)
Robinson	15637 (45.5%)	+ 2926 =	18563 (54.6%)

Robinson wins

Dublin N.C.	First Count	Second Count	

(Total poll 68.0%)

	First Count	Second Count
Currie	4752 (12.7%)	
Lenihan	16658 (44.5%)	+ 736 = 17394 (47.0%)
Robinson	16064 (42.9%)	+ 3521 = 19585 (53.0%)

Robinson wins

Dublin N.E.	First Count	Second Count
(Total poll 63.3%)		
Currie	3690 (10.9%)	
Lenihan	13939 (41.3%)	+ 598 = 14537 (43.6%)
Robinson	16082 (47.7%)	+ 2690 = 18772 (56.4%)

Robinson wins

Dublin N.W.	First Count	Second Count
(Total poll 58.3%)		
Currie	2795 (10.1%)	
Lenihan	11611 (42.0%)	+ 448 = 12059 (44.1%)
Robinson	13240 (47.9%)	+ 2041 = 15281 (55.9%)

Robinson wins

Dublin South	First Count	Second Count
(Total poll 67.5%)		
Currie	9646 (17.0%)	
Lenihan	17948 (31.7%)	+ 1382 = 19330 (34.6%)
Robinson	29103 (51.3%)	+ 7370 = 36473 (65.4%)

Robinson wins

Dublin S.C.	First Count	Second Count
(Total poll 60.2%)		
Currie	5578 (13.0%)	
Lenihan	16847 (39.3%)	+ 896 = 17743 (42.0%)
Robinson	20394 (47.6%)	+ 4123 = 24517 (58.0%)

Robinson wins

Dublin S.E.	First Count	Second Count
(Total poll 59.0%)		
Currie	5528 (16.6%)	
Lenihan	10573 (31.7%)	+ 785 = 11358 (34.7%)
Robinson	17262 (51.7%)	+ 4156 = 21418 (65.3%)

Robinson wins

Dublin S.W.	First Count	Second Count
(Total poll 55.7%)		
Currie	3661 (9.9%)	
Lenihan	15340 (41.7%)	+ 554 = 15894 (43.6%)
Robinson	17826 (48.4%)	+ 2747 = 20573 (56.4%)

Robinson wins

Dublin West	First Count	Second Count
(Total poll 61.3%)		
Currie	6439 (13.4%)	
Lenihan	21987 (45.6%)	+ 972 = 22959 (48.2%)
Robinson	19772 (41.0%)	+ 4896 = 24668 (51.8%)

Robinson wins

Dun Laoghaire	First Count	Second Count
(Total poll 65.0%)		
Currie	8957 (17.0%)	
Lenihan	14974 (28.4%)	+ 1319 = 16293 (31.4%)
Robinson	28815 (54.6%)	+ 6712 = 35527 (68.6%)

Robinson wins

Galway East	First Count	Second Count
(Total poll 65.1%)		
Currie	5629 (20.4%)	
Lenihan	13883 (50.4%)	+ 603 = 14486 (53.4%)
Robinson	8043 (29.2%)	+ 4608 = 12651 (46.6%)

Lenihan wins

Galway West	First Count	Second Count
(Total poll 59.3%)		
Currie	8094 (17.6%)	
Lenihan	18885 (41.1%)	+ 990 = 19875 (43.8%)
Robinson	18979 (41.3%)	+ 6494 = 25472 (56.2%)

Robinson wins

Kerry North	First Count	Second Count
(Total poll 64.0%)		
Currie	5192 (17.2%)	
Lenihan	13896 (45.9%)	+ 773 = 14669 (49.3%)
Robinson	11155 (36.9%)	+ 3941 = 15096 (50.7%)

Robinson wins

Kerry South	First Count	Second Count
(Total poll 66.6%)		
Currie	4891 (17.2%)	
Lenihan	14230 (50.0%)	+ 582 = 14812 (52.8%)
Robinson	9336 (32.8%)	+ 3902 = 13238 (47.2%)

Lenihan wins

Kildare	First Count	Second Count
(Total poll 63.1%)		
Currie	7701 (15.2%)	
Lenihan	21388 (42.2%)	+ 1105 = 22493 (45.0%)
Robinson	21638 (42.7%)	+ 5829 = 27467 (55.0%)

Robinson wins

Laois/Offaly	First Count	Second Count	
(Total poll 68.0%)			
Currie	8690 (17.1%)		
Lenihan	25635 (50.4%)	+ 1105 =	26740 (53.3%)
Robinson	16571 (32.6%)	+ 6826 =	23397 (46.7%)
Lenihan wins			

Limerick East	First Count	Second Count	
(Total poll 63.4%)			
Currie	7498 (17.6%)		
Lenihan	14583 (34.2%)	+ 1006 =	15589 (37.3%)
Robinson	20527 (48.2%)	+ 5708 =	26235 (62.7%)
Robinson wins			

Limerick West	First Count	Second Count	
(Total poll 70.6%)			
Currie	5955 (19.3%)		
Lenihan	16055 (52.2%)	+ 779 =	16834 (55.7%)
Robinson	8766 (28.5%)	+ 4614 =	13380 (44.3%)
Lenihan wins			

Longford/Westmeath	First Count	Second Count	
(Total poll 66.5%)			
Currie	7716 (18.7%)		
Lenihan	21860 (52.9%)	+ 1021 =	22881 (56.3%)
Robinson	11741 (28.4%)	+ 6054 =	17795 (43.7%)
Lenihan wins			

Louth	First Count	Second Count	
(Total poll 62.9%)			
Currie	5588 (14.1%)		
Lenihan	20134 (50.8%)	+ 936 =	21070 (53.9%)
Robinson	13894 (35.1%)	+ 4159 =	18053 (46.1%)
Lenihan wins			

Mayo East	First Count	Second Count	
(Total poll 67.8%)			
Currie	5023 (18.7%)		
Lenihan	11838 (44.2%)	+ 524 =	12362 (46.6%)
Robinson	9947 (37.1%)	+ 4215 =	14162 (53.4%)
Robinson wins			

Mayo West	First Count	Second Count	
(Total poll 65.1%)			
Currie	4706 (18.3%)		
Lenihan	12114 (47.1%)	+ 452 =	12566 (49.5%)
Robinson	8905 (34.6%)	+ 3940 =	12845 (50.5%)
Robinson wins			

Meath	First Count	Second Count	
(Total poll 63.2%)			
Currie	8174 (16.7%)		
Lenihan	23960 (48.9%)	+ 1162 =	25122 (52.2%)
Robinson	16818 (34.4%)	+ 6219 =	23037 (47.8%)

Lenihan wins

Roscommon	First Count	Second Count	
(Total poll 69.7%)			
Currie	6482 (23.0%)		
Lenihan	14454 (51.3%)	+ 731 =	15185 (54.9%)
Robinson	7223 (25.7%)	+ 5272 =	12495 (45.1%)

Lenihan wins

Sligo/Leitrim	First Count	Second Count	
(Total poll 65.5%)			
Currie	7794 (20.3%)		
Lenihan	18917 (49.3%)	+ 989 =	19906 (52.7%)
Robinson	11660 (30.4%)	+ 6222 =	17882 (47.3%)

Lenihan wins

Tipperary North	First Count	Second Count	
(Total poll 70.2%)			
Currie	5822 (20.0%)		
Lenihan	14373 (49.4%)	+ 746 =	15119 (52.9%)
Robinson	8926 (30.6%)	+ 4557 =	13483 (47.1%)

Lenihan wins

Tipperary South	First Count	Second Count	
(Total poll 67.9%)			
Currie	7227 (19.4%)		
Lenihan	17317 (46.4%)	+ 982 =	18299 (50.1%)
Robinson	12751 (34.2%)	+ 5463 =	18214 (49.9%)

Lenihan wins

Waterford	First Count	Second Count	
(Total poll 63.7%)			
Currie	6160 (15.9%)		
Lenihan	17236 (44.5%)	+ 934 =	18170 (47.7%)
Robinson	15359 (39.6%)	+ 4521 =	19880 (52.3%)

Robinson wins

Wexford	First Count	Second Count	
(Total poll 65.3%)			
Currie	7906 (16.9%)		
Lenihan	21790 (46.5%)	+ 1200 =	22990 (49.9%)
Robinson	17201 (36.7%)	+ 5857 =	23058 (50.1%)

Robinson wins

Wicklow (Total poll 62.2%)	First Count	Second Count
Currie	5891 (14.1%)	
Lenihan	16448 (39.4%)	+ 905 = 17353 (42.1%)
Robinson	19393 (46.5%)	+ 4449 = 23842 (57.9%)

Robinson wins

National (Total poll 64.1%)	First Count	Second Count
Currie	267902 (17.0%)	
Lenihan	694484 (44.1%)	+ 36798 = 731273 (47.2%)
Robinson	612265 (38.9%)	+205565 = 817830 (52.8%)

Robinson wins by 5.6%

Mary won twenty-five of the forty-one constituencies, in urban and rural areas. She took every constituency in the Dublin area, and all except one in Cork. All of the cities – Cork, Limerick, Waterford – fell to her. But so did Carlow, Kilkenny, North Kerry, and counties Kildare, Waterford, Wexford, and Wicklow. And sweetest of all, perhaps, she won both constituencies in County Mayo, her home country – and the political base of Padraig Flynn.

On a provincial basis, Mary won handsomely in the Dublin area (by 72,746 votes), and in Munster (by 27,593 votes). In so far as the rest of Leinster (other than Dublin city and county) was concerned, she won the south of Leinster, but Lenihan beat her in the north, and just shaded the region in overall terms by the tightest of margins – 50.05% to 49.95%. Out of 367,134 votes cast in Leinster, Lenihan won by just 370 votes! The only region he won convincingly was Connaught/Ulster – by 13,412 votes. But Mayo had stayed loyal to its own woman.

To those who were watching, the most remarkable feature of the victory was the transfer pattern, the most unique in any national election in the history of the State. After Currie was eliminated, just under one in ten of his votes were non-transferable. Of the rest, 77%

went to Robinson, and 13% to Lenihan – in other words, his second preferences went to Robinson by a factor of six to one. The lowest transfer she got anywhere was 69.9% in Donegal North East, and the highest were 83.7% and 83.9% in, of all places, the two Mayo constituencies. It seems that the people of Mayo were determined to elect *their* President!

For Fianna Fáil, the result was a terrible shock. Heartland after heartland fell to the Mary Robinson bandwagon, and their share of the vote was no better that the result they had achieved in the general election a year before. The strategy of running the most popular man in the party had come to nothing, and the financial cost had been almost two million pounds.

It's not known how much Fine Gael spent, but the result was a complete disaster. In only one constituency in Ireland did Austin Currie come higher than third, and the highest vote he managed anywhere was 21.2%. In overall terms, the party's votes dropped from 29% in the recent general election to 17% – a catastrophe by any standards.

The Robinson team spent the grand total of £220,000, and raised only £140,000 in the course of the campaign, leaving a deficit on polling day of £80,000. But what price should you pay to make history?

The presidential election of 1990 was a triumph in many ways. It was a triumph of dedication and commitment over the huge resources and bigger machines of the largest political parties in the State. It was a triumph of imagination and energy over the stale ideas of stuck-in-the-mud, complacent organisations. It was a triumph of style and substance.

It can never be forgotten that this victory was conceived in the first place by Dick Spring, who had the insight to choose a candidate who did not fit in with traditional thinking. There were many who doubted his wisdom for a long time – but he showed that political perceptions should never be taken for granted.

It was a victory for all the people who worked for Mary Robinson for months, with no pay and only the reward of believing in a dream and seeing it come true. Many of them will never see their names in print, but they all know what they did, and they all know that it was work well worth doing.

It was a victory for Mary's family – Nick, Tessa, William and Aubrey – who all made their own sacrifices and were throughout the main inspiration that Mary needed, her father Aubrey, her brothers and their families, and for a host of close friends who all put their shoulders to the wheel in what became a cause bigger than family.

It was a triumph for Mary herself, a woman who had rediscovered the road map of her own country, who had fallen in love with that country and it with her, and whose independence, fortitude, and courage were the perfect qualifications for the office she now holds.

Above all, it was a triumph for the people of Ireland, who took this election seriously when there were many who did not want them to; who looked to the future rather than the past; who cast aside the prejudices and the traditions of old; who thought for themselves and who chose for themselves Mary Robinson, a President with a Purpose.

"Victory and valediction"

Although it was vital to get the news of Mary's election to Katmandu, it proved to be impossible, until word of mouth did the trick.

Ann Lane has been Mary's secretary and close friend for twenty one years, and no-one worked harder than she did during the campaign. But there was a problem. It has been one of the great ambitions of Ann's life to see Mount Everest, and for years she had been planning a trip, together with a group of friends. A hike in the Himalayas is not quite the same as a holiday in Torremolinos – apart from the logistics of clothes, luggage, first aid equipment, and "shots", there is enormous bureaucracy involved. Trips to Mount Everest, as a result, take years to organise, and are impossible to postpone for a couple of weeks.

Anne left for Mount Everest on October 24th, when it still looked as if Mary Robinson could win, rather than would win. As Mary told her, "Now we both have big mountains to climb!" That was the last Ann heard of the campaign for some time.

It had been Ann's original plan to hike to the base camp, 17,000 feet high on Everest. At 15,000 feet, she got altitude sickness, a condition that can kill if the hiker keeps climbing. She had to leave the group, and make her way back down, with a young sherpa to guide her, to Tyanboche Monastery. As you go back down, the altitude sickness eases, and by the time she got there, she was feeling better, although she still had to rest for several days. Somewhere in the Himalayas today, there's a young sherpa guide who still wears a sweatshirt with Mary Robinson's name and logo on it – that was the present Ann gave him.

It was the 18th of November, in Katmandu, when Ann met an Irish woman who had just arrived after a long trek from Delhi. The woman had rung her husband in Ireland before leaving the Indian capital, to be brought up-to-date with all the news from home. "By the way," her husband had told, "your woman Mary Robinson just won the presidential election."

Anne couldn't believe the news, and couldn't wait to tell the rest of the group when they got back from base camp. But when they arrived, a couple of days later, they already knew. At 17,000 feet up the side of Mount Everest, the BBC World Service had come in crystal clear on their transistor radio, and it had broadcast the news to the world.

Still she wanted to see it in print, before she could fully believe it. Maybe there'd be an English newspaper in the airport in Dubai, which was their first stop on the way home. But the only newspaper available was the local *Dubai News*. Idly flicking through it, she found the confirmation she was looking for – a colour photograph of the new President of Ireland, accompanying an interview with one of the wire services in which she outlined her hopes for the next seven years.

There was another surprise awaiting Ann Lane when she got home. Declan and Barry had arranged that she would be met by a long, black, presidential limousine, and that was what she was driven home in.

There were a lot of people who found it difficult to believe that Mary had actually been elected. The impossible had been achieved. Mary had not gone just to the foothills – she had scaled Everest's peak. And she had done it against all the odds, and as the candidate for a different set of values, values that had never prevailed in any national election before.

The news spread worldwide. Throughout the campaign it had been said again and again, especially by Fine Gael people, that the election result would make a statement about Ireland and the Irish to the rest of the world. Many in the Robinson campaign recoiled from that kind of language, believing it to be something of an affront to voters. Mary herself preferred to believe that, on the day, the Irish people would make a statement about themselves to themselves.

But one way or the other, the rest of the world understood Ireland to have made a huge leap forward. Newspapers and magazines in virtually every country in the world carried the story. Mary Robinson had joined a very small number of women – still no more than a dozen in the twentieth century history of the world! – who had been elected to their country's highest office. It was, quite properly, seen as historic.

In Ireland, some of the repercussions were immediate, and others will take a lot longer. Before Mary had left the RDS after the official declaration, a Fine Gael back-bencher had put down a motion of no confidence in the party leader Alan Dukes. By the following Wednesday Dukes had resigned, and was immediately replaced by his deputy leader John Bruton.

In the very first speech made by Bruton as leader of Fine Gael, he chose to re-open the debate about divorce in Ireland, and to raise the possibility of another divorce referendum in the near future. Within days the Taoiseach Mr Haughey was telling the Dáil that he was prepared to consider the publication of a White Paper on the whole subject of divorce, while pointing out that a lot of work would need to be done to prepare public opinion to debate the area properly. Clearly, despite her election to an office outside party politics, Mary was still setting the agenda!

At the first meeting of his party's Administrative Council after the election, Dick Spring said that the election of Mary Robinson had established that there was room in Irish politics for the values that she represented. He predicted that Labour would seek to fill that room by updating its policies and revising its structures to take account of the mood for change, and for more openness, that Mary had revealed.

Within a traumatised Fianna Fáil party, rumblings of dissent began to emerge. Five members of the party's National Executive Committee harshly criticised the role played by the Taoiseach, and called on him to resign. Lenihan himself and several other senior figures in the party attacked Fianna Fáil's junior coalition partners, the Progressive Democrats, who had been responsible in the eyes of many Fianna Fáil people for forcing the sacking of Brian Lenihan from the Cabinet, and many of whose members had worked for Mary during the campaign. The party embarked on a period of soul-searching which seemed certain to lead ultimately to new policies, as well to the departure of its present leader.

What had started out as a boring, predictable election, with Mary Robinson being seen by many as a worthy but no-hope idea, had ended up as a cataclysmic event for Irish politics. The establishment had been shaken to its roots by the election of a young radical woman who had set out seven months earlier to capture the hearts and minds of the Irish people. Unnoticed by her political enemies until it was too late, and with only the help of small political parties and a host of committed individuals, she had done it. In her own words in the RDS, she had "rocked the system".

On the evening that Mary was declared elected, national and international media gathered in Jury's Hotel, just down the road from the RDS, to cover a press conference that Mary had promised to give after the declaration. The hotel had made one of its suites available free of charge, and had also provided four bottles of champagne on ice for the President-elect. Anne Byrne was offering everyone who came in a red rose. It was a chaotic scene, with reporters, cameramen and photographers jostling for the best angles.

One of the Robinson committee stood at the back, savouring the atmosphere. Halfway through the press conference, he turned to the person standing beside him, who was Liz Allman, Ruairi Quinn's wife. She noticed that there were tears in his eyes. "I've just realised," he whispered to her, "that's *our* President." She knew exactly what he meant.

"The Fifth Province"

In its seven hundred and fifty years of history, Dublin Castle has seen many momentous occasions, though, for many of those involved, there has never been an occasion as joyous as the inauguration of Mary Robinson.

Besieged by "Silken Thomas" in 1534, used as a prison for Red Hugh O'Donnell in 1592, burned down and rebuilt in 1684, the Castle has had a tumultuous story. The year after it was rebuilt, it was occupied by James II, for one night, in his hasty retreat from the Battle of the Boyne. In one of the more grisly incidents associated with the Castle, in the wake of the 1798 Rising, the bodies of insurgents, many of which had been hacked to death by sabres, were laid out in the Castle yard as a warning to the citizens of Dublin. Four years later, Robert Emmet made an abortive effort to capture the Castle, and was hanged for his pains.

Throughout the nineteenth century, the Castle was the seat of British power in Ireland, and became a hated symbol, especially during the Great Famine years of 1846-8 when, as hundreds of thousands of people starved to death throughout the country, the viceregal court located in the Castle was maintained, and the endless round of receptions, balls, and levees continued uninterrupted. The last attack on the Castle came during the 1916 Rising, when a party of armed Volunteers tried unsuccessfully to take it over. After the Rising, James Connolly was held prisoner in the Castle for some time before being taken to Kilmainham Jail to be shot.

Six years later, in 1922, the Castle was handed over peacefully by the Lord Lieutenant to the Provisional Government of Ireland. No longer the scene of power, Dublin Castle has nevertheless witnessed many colourful scenes in the years since Ireland's independence, and has been the site of every presidential inauguration since the first one.

Mary Robinson had spent many memorable days there during the New Ireland Forum in 1984, when, as a member of the Labour Party delegation, she had made a considerable impact on the report that that body had produced, with its analysis of the nationalist issue and its various options for progress in relation to the troubled issue of Northern Ireland. Along with other members of the Forum, she had insisted on ensuring that the options for unity outlined in the New Ireland Forum report were not confined exclusively to the three options spelled out in detail in the report.

One of the most dramatic confrontations that had occurred in Dublin Castle during the deliberations of the Forum had been that between Mary and the representatives of the Catholic hierarchy, when they had come to spell out their position in relation to the possible changes that a united Ireland might bring. She had politely but firmly questioned the bishops present, in a session that was occasionally tense, about their reluctance to wholeheartedly endorse the pluralism that was a part of her conviction.

Among the bishops who went to Dublin Castle that day was Dr Cathal Daly, then Bishop of Down and Conor. In the course of the presidential campaign, Dr Daly was himself elevated to the high office of Catholic Primate of All Ireland, and now he, along with other Church representatives, was coming to do honour to the woman he had once faced across a table in the same castle.

If Mary appreciated the irony inherent in the situation, nothing of it showed as she made her entrance to St Patrick's Hall, where the cream of the nation's establishment was waiting. Most members of the Oireachtas were there, together with senior judges – before most of whom Mary Robinson had appeared as an advocate – ambassadors, prelates, mayors and chairpersons of local authorities, representatives of the universities and other seats of learning, and a host of other dignitaries.

And among them, the people whom Mary had invited as her own personal guests. Some of them were there, as well as in their personal capacities, to represent organisations to which Mary was committed – symbols of her continuing intention to represent those "whose voice is weak". Mary had ensured that the Council for the Status of Women and the Women's Political Association were there, as well as the National Campaign for the Homeless, the Focus on Disability Group, Focuspoint, and others.

There were some who represented no organisation, but whose presence spoke volumes about Mary's commitment. Gordon Wilson, whose daughter Marie had died in the Remembrance Day bombing in Enniskillen, and whose courage and charity had impressed the world, sat quietly throughout the ceremony, his presence a testimony to reconciliation. But politicians from all sides of the divide in Northern Ireland had come too – John Hume, Ken Magennis, and John Alderdice – the leaders of public opinion in a divided community, come together to celebrate one who had promised to extend the hand of friendship and love across all divisions.

And finally, there were some in the audience whose qualification was that they had helped and supported Mary throughout the previous seven months, contributing, each in their own way, to the moment of Mary's inauguration. Darina Allen, Brenda O'Hanlon, Bride Rosney – who was to become the first Special Advisor to a President in the history of the State – all were there, with members of Mary's family and many other friends, to savour and share in the moment they had all worked for.

The outgoing Council of State, with the Government and representatives of the Churches, were already seated on the dais at the top of St Patrick's Hall when Mary, accompanied by the Tánaiste, entered. She was led up the aisle through the middle of the great hall by two army officers, followed closely by Nick, who was accompanied by the Minister for Foreign Affairs. Everyone in the hall stood as the party made its way to the dais, and remained standing until Mary took her seat.

The Taoiseach began the ceremony by calling on the Church representatives to commence the inter-denominational service of prayer that preceded the taking of the oath. And then it was the turn of the Chief Justice, Mr Justice Thomas Finlay, to read the Declaration of Office to the President-elect.

Mary already knew it by heart. She had repeated this vow again and again during the campaign – a vow that, in her own words, she would be honoured to take and determined to uphold. In her strong voice, that only occasionally betrayed the nervousness she must have felt, and that nevertheless echoed around the hall, she repeated the words in Irish that the Chief Justice read to her in the first official language:

In the presence of Almighty God, I, Mary Robinson, do solemnly and sincerely promise and declare that I will maintain the Constitution of Ireland and uphold its laws, that I will fulfil my duties faithfully and conscientiously in accordance with the Constitution and the law, and that I will dedicate my abilities to the service and welfare of the people of Ireland. May God direct me and sustain me.

When she had finished, the Chief Justice offered her the Declaration for her signature. Turning to the audience, he announced: "The President has entered upon her office in accordance with the Constitution."

Then he presented her with her seal of office, the Presidential Seal. Mary Robinson, whom no-one had given any hope of winning the election in April, was now the seventh President of Ireland, and the first woman ever to hold the office.

The Taoiseach spoke briefly and graciously, assuring Ireland's new President of the support and loyalty of the Government and every citizen. Then it was Mary's turn. Standing at the podium before this expectant and attentive audience, she made her first address to the people of Ireland as their elected first citizen.

❧

Citizens of Ireland, *mná na hÉireann agus fir na hÉireann*, you have chosen me to represent you and I am humbled by and grateful for your trust.

The Ireland I will be representing is a new Ireland, open, tolerant, inclusive. Many of you who voted for me did so without sharing all my views. This, I believe, is a significant signal of change, a sign, however modest, that we have already passed the threshold to a new, pluralist Ireland.

The recent revival of an old concept of the Fifth Province expresses this emerging Ireland of tolerance and empathy. The old Irish term for province is *coicead*, meaning a "fifth"; and yet, as everyone knows, there are only four geographical provinces on this island. So where is the fifth? The Fifth Province is not anywhere here or there, north or south, east or west. It is a place within each one of us – that place that is open to the other, that swinging door which allows us to venture out and others to venture in. Ancient legends divided Ireland into four quarters and a "middle", although they differed about the location of this middle or Fifth Province. While Tara was the political centre of Ireland, tradition has it that this Fifth Province acted as a second centre, a necessary balance. If I am a symbol of anything I would like to be a symbol of this reconciling and healing Fifth Province.

My primary role as President will be to represent this State. But the State is not the only model of community with which Irish people can and do identify. Beyond our State there is a vast community of Irish emigrants extending not only across our neighbouring island – which has provided a home away from home for several Irish generations – but also throughout the continents of North America, Australia and of course Europe itself. There are over 70 million people living on this globe who claim Irish descent. I will be proud to represent them. And I would like to see Áras an Uachtaráin, my official residence, serve – on something of an annual basis – as a place where our emigrant communities could send representatives for a get-together of the extended Irish family abroad.

There is another level of community which I will represent. Not just the national, not just the global, but the local community. Within our State there are a growing number of local and regional communities determined to express their own creativity, identity, heritage and initiative in new and exciting ways. In my travels around Ireland

I have found local community groups thriving on a new sense of self-confidence and self-empowerment. Whether it was groups concerned with adult education, employment initiative, women's support, local history and heritage, environmental concern or community culture, one of the most enriching discoveries was to witness the extent of this local empowerment at work.

As President I will seek to the best of my abilities to promote this growing sense of local participatory democracy, this emerging movement of self development and self expression which is surfacing more and more at grassroots level. This is the face of modern Ireland.

Ba mhaith liom a rá go bhfuair mé taithneamh agus pléisiúr as an taisteal a rinne mé le míosa anuas ar fuaid na hÉireann. Is fíor álainn agus iontach an tír atá againn, agus is álainn an pobal iad muintir na hÉireann.

Fuair mé teachtaireacht ón bpobal seo agus mé ag dul timpeall: "Teastaíonn Uachtarán uainn gur féidir linn bheith bródúil aisti, ach, níos mó ná sin, gur féidir linn bheith bródúil lena chéile – toisc gur Éireannaigh sinn, agus go bhfuil traidisiúin agus cultúr álainn againn".

Is cuid an-tábhachtach don gcultúr sin an Ghaeilge – an teanga bheo – fé mar atá á labhairt sa Ghaeltacht agus ag daoine eile ar fuaid na hÉireann.

Tá aistear eile le déanamh anois agam – aistear cultúrtha, leis an saibhreas iontach atá sa teanga Ghaeilge a bhaint amach díom féin.

Tá súil agam go leanfaidh daoine eile mé atá ar mo nós fhéin – beagán as cleachtadh sa Ghaeilge – agus go raghaimíd ar aghaidh le chéile le taithneamh agus pléisiúr a fháil as ár dteanga álainn féin.

Translation

[I want to say how much I enjoyed travelling around Ireland over the last few months. Ours is a truly beautiful country and the Irish people are a wonderful race.

I got a message from the people that they wanted a President they could be proud of, but more than that, that we could take pride together

– in our Irishness and our wonderful heritage and culture.

The Irish language is an important part of that culture, as spoken in the Gaeltacht areas and around the country. I am about to embark on another journey – a cultural voyage of discovery of the wealth and beauty of the Irish language. I hope others who, like myself, are somewhat out of practice, will join me on this journey, and that we will progress together to enjoy to the full our own beautiful language.]

The best way we can contribute to a new integrated Europe of the 1990s is by having a confident sense of our Irishness. Here again we must play to our strengths – take full advantage of our vibrant cultural resources in music, art, drama, literature and film; value the role of our educators; promote and preserve our unique environmental and geographical resources of relatively pollution-free lakes, rivers, land-scapes and seas; encourage and publicly support local initiative projects in aquaculture, forestry, fishing, alternative energy and smallscale technology.

Looking outwards from Ireland, I would like on your behalf to contribute to the international protection and promotion of human rights. One of our greatest national resources has always been, and still is, our ability to serve as a moral and political conscience in world affairs. We have a long history of providing spiritual, cultural, and social assistance to other countries in need – most notably in Latin America, Africa and other Third World countries. And we can continue to promote these values by taking principled and inde-pendent stands on issues of international importance.

As the elected President of this small democratic country I assume office at a vital moment in Europe's history. Ideological boundaries that have separated East from West are withering away at an astound-ing pace. Eastern countries are seeking to participate as full partners in a restructured and economically buoyant Europe. The stage is set for a new common European home based on respect for human rights, pluralism, tolerance and openness to new ideas. The European Con-vention on Human Rights – one of the finest achievements of the Council of Europe – is asserting itself as the natural Constitution for the new Europe. These developments have created one of the major challenges for the 1990s.

If it is time, as Joyce's Stephen Dedalus remarked, that the Irish began to forge in the smithy of our souls "the uncreated conscience of our race" – might we not also take on the still "uncreated conscience" of the wider international community? Is it not time that the small started believing again that it is beautiful, that the periphery can rise up and speak out on equal terms with the centre, that the most outlying island community of the European Community really has something "strange and precious" to contribute to the sea-change presently sweeping through the entire continent of Europe? As a native of Ballina, one of the most western towns in the most western province of the most western nation in Europe, I want to say – "the West's awake".

I turn now to another place close to my heart, Northern Ireland. As the elected choice of the people of this part of our island I want to extend the hand of friendship and of love to both communities in the other part. And I want to do this with no hidden agenda, no strings attached. As the person chosen by you to symbolise this Republic and to project our self image to others, I will seek to encourage mutual understanding and tolerance between all the different communities sharing this island.

In seeking to do this I shall rely to a large extent on symbols. But symbols are what unite and divide people. Symbols give us our identity, our self image, our way of explaining ourselves to ourselves and to others. Symbols in turn determine the kinds of stories we tell; and the stories we tell determine the kind of history we make and remake. I want Áras an Uachtaráin to be a place where people can tell diverse stories – in the knowledge that there is someone there to listen.

I want this Presidency to promote the telling of stories – stories of celebration through the arts and stories of conscience and of social justice. As a woman, I want women who have felt themselves outside history to be written back into history, in the words of Eavan Boland, "finding a voice where they found a vision".

May God direct me so that my Presidency is one of justice, peace and love. May I have the fortune to preside over an Ireland at a time of exciting transformation when we enter a new Europe where old wounds can be healed, a time when, in the words of Seamus Heaney, "hope and history rhyme". May it be a Presidency where I the President can sing to you, citizens of Ireland, the joyous refrain of the 14th century Irish poet as recalled by W.B.Yeats:

"I am of Ireland . . . come dance with me in Ireland".

Go raibh míle maith agaibh go léir.

❦

There was sustained applause from every person present when Mary had finished. Mary Robinson had embarked on a new phase of her life, and she had done so with dignity and style. Ireland too had entered on a new phase. Back in June, Mary had written to her supporters that *"to return an elected working President supported by a mandate from the people will literally change the shape of Irish politics and signal a more open and pluralist society."*

The signal had been sent, and the future had opened up. Irish politics will never be the same again.